BOOK 3

PATTERNS IN SPELLING

Patterns with Consonant Blends and Digraphs

TIM BROWN & DEBORAH F. KNIGHT

NEW READERS PRESS
Publishing Division of Laubach Literacy International
Syracuse, New York

About the Authors

Deborah Knight began her teaching career in the early 1970s and has taught both reading and English in urban, suburban, and rural settings. Since 1984, Ms. Knight has served as the Coordinator of the Learning Disabilities Assistance Program at Onondaga Community College in Syracuse, New York. Working closely with these OCC students, she has helped them to develop strategies for improving their reading, writing, spelling, and study skills.

Tim Brown has worked with developing and remedial readers and writers since 1978. He teaches courses in spelling as well as freshman composition and literature at Onondaga Community College. He also serves as Senior Professional Tutor at the college's Writing Skills Center, where he has a special interest in teaching spelling to developing and remedial writers and ESL students.

ON THE COVER: A quilt entitled *Rhythm/Color: Morris Men,* 99½" x 99½", by Michael James. This work of art appeared in *The Art Quilt* exhibit and book of the same name. It is reproduced here through the courtesy of The Quilt Digest Press.

ISBN 0-88336-105-1

New Readers Press
Publishing Division of Laubach Literacy International
Box 131, Syracuse, New York 13210

Printed in the United States of America

Project Editor: Christina M. Jagger
Manuscript Editor: Mary Hutchison
Designed by Chris Steenwerth
Cover by Chris Steenwerth
Illustrations by Christine Patsos-Kocak
Composition by Anne Hyde
Layout Artist: Joanne Groth

9 8 7 6 5 4 3 2

Table of Contents

Glossary of Terms

affix A word element that carries meaning and is attached to a root word. Prefixes and suffixes are affixes; for example, *de-* and *-ful* in *delightful.*

blend The joining together of two or more sounds with each sound still being heard; for example, /tr/ in *trade.*

C A symbol representing any consonant.

compound word A word formed by combining two or more words. Compound words can be closed (*greenhouse*), hyphenated (*red-letter*), or open (*yellow jacket*).

diacritical mark A mark added to a letter to show how to pronounce the letter; for example, the straight line over a vowel to show a long vowel sound.

digraph A pair of letters that represents one sound; for example, *ch* making the sound /ch/ in *chain* and *ea* making the sound /ē/ in *sea.*

family A letter pattern or sequence such as *ine* in *fine, mine*, and *combine*. The pattern usually forms a common syllable ending and is composed of a vowel or vowel combination plus the consonant(s) that go with it.

homonym One of a pair or more of words having the same sound but different meanings and often different spellings; for example, *tail* and *tale.*

mnemonic A device, such as a rhyme, used to aid in remembering something.

pattern A recurrent, usually predictable sequence of letters. Patterns occur in common syllables (e.g., *ope*) as well as in prefixes, suffixes, roots, and compound words. Spelling rules also produce patterns.

prefix A word element that carries meaning and is attached to the beginning of a root word; for example, *pre-* in *prepaid.*

schwa A vowel sound that usually occurs in unstressed syllables in English as heard in the first syllable of *against*; also the symbol (ə) often used to represent the sound.

sight word A word that is not phonetically predictable; also any word for which students have not had the phonics to enable them to spell the word phonetically.

suffix A word element that carries meaning and is attached to the end of a root word; for example, *-less* in *speechless.*

syllable A spoken unit of uninterrupted sound containing one vowel sound producing either a word (e.g., *pay*) or a distinct part of a word (e.g., *pay* or *ment* in *payment*); the letters producing that sound in the word.

V A symbol representing any vowel.

Style Notes

/x/ A letter between slashes indicates a sound rather than a spelling; for instance /b/ is the sound produced by the letter *b*.

/ĭ/ A curved mark (breve) over a vowel indicates the short vowel sound.

/i/ No diacritical mark also indicates the short vowel sound.

/ī/ A straight line (macron) over a vowel indicates the long vowel sound.

/ə/ This indicates the schwa sound.

S: This indicates something said by the student.

T: This indicates something said by the teacher or tutor.

1. Overview of the Series

Patterns in Spelling provides students with a powerful, systematic method of learning to spell by stressing the patterns that are regularly found in English words. Many patterns included in this series are word families composed of syllables or syllable endings—for example, *ot*, *ight*, *ed*, and *ouse*. Other patterns are based on consonant blends and digraphs. This approach emphasizes the regularities of spelling more strongly than does a purely phonics-based approach. It is highly effective with adults who are just learning to read and write as well as with adults and older teens who may know how to read but who have failed to learn to spell using a more traditional, straight-phonics approach.

The Pattern Approach

In the pattern approach, students learn to perceive that words contain a common pattern plus other letters. This method simplifies the task of learning to spell. Rather than studying sequences of individual letters, students study the spelling of the pattern as a unit. At the same time, students learn the pronunciation of the pattern. For instance, in Lesson 18 of Book 2, students study the *ight* pattern, learning that the spelling unit *i-g-h-t* makes the sound unit /īt/ and that /īt/ is spelled *i-g-h-t*. Then they study several representative words containing the pattern. Instead of having to learn the sequence of five letters to spell *light*, they learn a two-part sequence: *l* plus the *ight* pattern.

The pattern approach simplifies learning to spell the representative words presented in the lessons. It also provides students with an effective tool to predict the spelling of other words containing a particular sound unit. For instance, in Lesson 6 of Book 1, students study the *ill* pattern, learning that *ill* makes the sound /ĭl/ and that /ĭl/ is spelled *i-l-l*. They also study four representative words. But once students know that /ĭl/ is spelled *i-l-l* at the end of words, they should be able to spell other words belonging to this family. To reinforce this concept, they are asked to write nine words ending with the *ill* pattern later in the lesson.

The Discovery Approach

Throughout the series students are given exercises designed to help them discover patterns and rules. For instance, this method is used when students are learning about doubling a final consonant or dropping the final *e* before adding an ending beginning with a vowel. This inductive approach is in direct contrast to the usual approach of giving students a rule first and having them memorize it and then apply it. We believe that students are more likely to remember the pattern because they have figured it out for themselves.

Three Modes of Learning to Spell

This series integrates three ways of learning to spell—hearing, seeing, and writing the words. As students use these three modes to learn the spelling of a word, they are simultaneously developing three memories for the word—their memory for the way the word sounds, their memory for the way the word looks, and their memory for how it feels to write the word. By using three modes instead of only one, they learn the word more thoroughly. And when they need to spell the word, they have three ways to access its correct spelling.

Spelling as a Means to an End

When students are learning to spell, it is helpful to concentrate on words in isolation. Thus a number of exercises in this series deal only with the correct spelling of words. But in real life, spelling is generally only one element of a more complex writing task. So this series also includes various types of writing activities that students encounter in school, at home, and on the job. These activities are designed to help students transfer the spelling skills they are learning to real-life situations.

The Components of the Series

This series contains four student books, four teacher's editions of the student books, and a diagnostic/placement test. Each of the four books emphasizes one aspect of spelling: short vowels, long vowels, consonant blends and digraphs, and other vowel sounds.

Book 1: Patterns with Short Vowels presents word families containing short vowels. Common syllable consonant endings are grouped with the short vowel sounds to produce the word families. The vowels are presented in the order: *i, u, e, o, a*. The non-alphabetic order separates short vowel sounds that sound similar, particularly short *e* and *i*, to make it easier for students to learn and discriminate between them.

Book 2: Patterns with Long Vowels presents word families containing the long vowels: *a*, *e*, *i*, and *o*. Long *u*, with its two sounds, is presented in Book 4. The most common patterns for spelling long vowel sounds are presented, along with strategies for learning homonyms and correct spellings when more than one would be phonetically correct.

Book 3: Patterns with Consonant Blends and Digraphs presents beginning and ending consonant blends, digraphs that can be positioned at either the beginning or end of syllables, and silent consonants.

Book 4: Patterns with Other Vowel Sounds and Spellings presents word families containing vowel sounds that are more difficult to spell. These include less common spellings of long and short vowel sounds, *r*-controlled vowels, and other vowel sounds such as /oi/.

The teacher's editions provide teaching suggestions, unit tests, and reduced replicas of the student pages with answers filled in.

The diagnostic/placement test is designed to determine which prerequisite spelling skills students possess and which they lack, and to help you place students in the proper book in the series. The test can be administered to either an individual or a group. Specific descriptions of the subtests and their use and interpretation are found in the teacher's edition of the diagnostic test.

2. Introduction to Book 3

Book 3 of *Patterns in Spelling* presents the most common initial and final consonant blends, digraphs, and silent consonant patterns. Initial two-letter blends are presented in Unit 1. Unit 2 deals with the digraphs *sh, ch, ph, th*, and *wh*, and suffixes that contain the /sh/ and /ch/ sounds. Initial three-letter blends are presented next, followed by ending blends in Units 4 and 5. Unit 6 deals with consonant pairs and clusters that contain silent consonants.

Several spelling strategies are introduced in Book 3, including how to discriminate between similar sounds, how to use apostrophes, and how to remember silent consonants in words. Practice is provided in using possessive and reflexive pronouns and in forming compound words, ordinal numbers, comparatives, and superlatives. Additional patterns for adding endings are introduced as well. Most of the lessons in Book 3 also provide students with opportunities for free writing.

In addition, Book 3 reviews several spelling strategies and skills introduced in Books 1 and 2: choosing the correct spelling from phonetically correct alternatives or homonym pairs, recognizing common syllable types, writing words of two or more syllables, finding root words, and using guide words to find words in the dictionary. Several patterns for adding endings are also reviewed, including dropping a final silent *e* when adding an ending that starts with a vowel and adding endings to words that end in a consonant plus *y* and to words that end in *f* or *fe*.

Using the Dictionary

It is important that students know the meanings of all of the words they learn to spell. Some students may not be familiar with all of the representative words in Book 3. They may also be unfamiliar with some of the words they form in the word building and adding endings exercises. Help students to develop the habit of looking up the meanings of unfamiliar words.

Some students may need reinforcement activities to improve their dictionary skills. If any students continue to have trouble with alphabetization, for instance, you can provide additional practice by having them alphabetize the words in word dictation exercises.

Unfamiliar Vowel Spellings

Some of the representative words in Book 3 contain vowel sounds and spellings that are covered in Book 4 of this series. These words are included because they are good examples of words that contain the blends and digraphs being presented. If some of your students have trouble learning to spell words containing vowel spellings they have not yet studied, have them concentrate on learning the common words that they use regularly. Strategies for learning the less regular vowel spellings are the focus of Book 4.

The Glossary and Style Notes

A glossary of terms and an explanation of the symbols used in this book are found on page four of this book. They are also included on the last page of the student text. As you are introducing students to Book 3, draw their attention to this reference material and discuss the terms as they encounter them in their lessons.

3. How to Use the Series

Patterns in Spelling is designed to make students aware that the spelling of the English language is actually quite regular, although complex. For this series to be successful in teaching students how to spell, you need to accept this premise and emphasize the regularity of the language.

The four workbooks in this series are designed to be used sequentially. Administer the diagnostic/placement test to determine which book each student should start in.

Students should not try to learn the spelling of phonetic patterns before they can sight-read words containing those patterns. If your students are learning to read as well as learning to spell, be sure they have been introduced to the necessary phonics in their reading. The order in which the word families are introduced in *Patterns in Spelling* basically corresponds to the sequence found in the *Laubach Way to Reading*, *Focus on Phonics*, and the *Challenger Adult Reading Series.*

The American Heritage Dictionary is used as the primary reference dictionary for this series. Since dictionaries are not uniform in their use of diacritical marks, some translation of our dictionary exercises may be necessary if your students are using another dictionary.

The Recommended Lesson Format

Before beginning to teach a lesson, you should carefully examine the blends, representative words, and lesson notes. In addition, you should develop any additional practice exercises you anticipate might be necessary.

Exactly how you decide to use these lessons will be determined by the number of students you have, the level of your students, the number of times you meet with students each week, and other variables. The following format is suggested for use with a group of students who are all working on the same lesson. In general, it is recommended that each lesson be taught over three class periods. Here is an overview of the suggested three-day format.

Day 1

1. Give a pretest on the sight words and then go over the sight words.
2. Present the listening exercise which deals with the representative words.
3. Complete all exercises related to the representative words and sight words except for the writing sentences exercise.
4. Assign studying the sight words and representative words as homework.

Day 2

1. Review the sight words and give a practice quiz on them.
2. Do the listening exercise again.
3. Introduce the other material presented in the lesson and complete the corresponding exercises either in class or for homework.
4. Assign as homework preparing for spelling quizzes on both the sight words and the representative words.

Day 3

1. Do the listening exercise once more.
2. Review new material introduced in the lesson and go over any exercises done for homework.
3. Complete the writing sentences exercise.
4. Give two graded spelling quizzes for the lesson—one on the sight words and the other on selected representative words introduced in the lesson.

Day 1 in Detail

1. Introduce the Sight Words

Many lessons in the series contain sight words—words that are not phonetically predictable or words for which the phonics necessary to spell them have not yet been introduced. Some words which appear as sight words early in the series will become predictable when the word families to which these sight words belong are introduced.

Remember that the two major steps to achieving the correct spelling of a sight word are: 1. remembering that the spelling of the word is not predictable in most cases and 2. recalling and producing the correct spelling.

Begin each lesson with a pretest of the sight words. Give the pretest before students have looked at the sight word list. Instruct students to leave three blank lines between each word. To give the pretest:

1. Say each sight word.
2. Use it in a simple sentence.
3. Say the sight word again.

Next have students open their books to the lesson and correct the pretest.

1. For each misspelled word, have the students underline any parts spelled correctly. This will help students to realize how much of each word they already know how to spell.
2. For each sight word, have the students write the correct spelling three times in a column to the right, even if the spelling in the pretest was correct. Students should say the word as they write it. In a classroom setting this can be conducted as a group activity.
3. When appropriate, help students to develop memory devices for difficult words. Do this by having students relate the sight words to words they already know how to spell. For example, *weight* becomes relatively easy to learn if the end spelling is associated with *eight*, an early sight word; *only* won't be misspelled *ownly* if its meaning and spelling are associated with the related word *one*. Make sure students write the memory devices near the list of sight words in their books. Do not have students develop memory devices for words that do not give them trouble.

Do not spend too much time on the sight words. The next activity, the listening exercise, is the most important part of the lesson.

2. Present the Listening Exercise

The listening exercise, Exercise 1 in each lesson, is core to this series. It teaches students to develop a systematic approach to analyzing words.

The listening exercise uses a variety of modes—seeing the words, hearing the words, and spelling the words—to help students to learn them. As students examine each blend or digraph, they follow a four-step process:

Step 1: They listen to the pronunication of the blend and then they spell the blend.

Step 2: They listen to the spelling of the blend and then they give the pronunication of the blend.

Step 3: They listen to each representative word, one at a time. They spell the blend and then the other sound(s) in the word.

Step 4: They listen to the word and then they spell the whole word.

A model of how to present the listening exercise is given in Lesson 1. Study this model and faithfully follow it. In general, we believe that you know your students best and should adapt materials to meet their needs and your teaching style. In the case of the listening exercise, however, you must adhere to the procedure if this approach is to be effective.

Notice that the words in each column are arranged so that the blend in each word lines up. This was done to help train students to see the blend in each word. You should point this out to your students.

As you are going over the representative words, concentrate on the shorter words in each list. The longer words are included to show students that the blends they are learning will help them to spell more complex words and to give them practice in recognizing the sounds in words of two or more syllables. Be sure that your students understand that the words listed are representative words and that usually there are many more words that contain each blend.

3. Do Exercises Related to Representative Words and Sight Words

Have students complete the one or two exercises related to the representative words and sight words that follow the listening exercise. The lesson notes explain how to do these exercises. In some exercises, you will have to dictate words to students. They can complete other exercises by themselves or in small groups.

As students are working on the exercises, observe what they are doing. If you see a student making errors in an exercise, correct the student quickly before he has a chance to reinforce a misconception.

4. Assign Homework

Have students study the sight words and the representative words for homework. Teach students to use the four-step methods outlined on the next page.

As you are introducing these methods, point out the similarities and differences between the steps for studying sight words and those for studying representative words. Help students to practice the methods during class until they have learned them. You may photocopy these instructions and give them to students.

How to Study Sight Words

1. Say the word.
- Listen for the consonant and vowel sounds.

2. Look at the word.
- Study the sequence of letters. Note the letters that spell the sounds.
- Pay special attention to the part of the word you misspelled on the pretest. If you have a memory device for that word, study it.

3. Think about the word.
- Think about how it sounds.
- Think about how it looks.
- Think about the memory device, if you have one.

4. Write the word.
- Ask yourself, "Does the word look right?"
- Check the spelling of the word.
- Write the word again if you are not sure of the spelling.

How to Study Representative Words

1. Say the word.
- Train yourself to listen for the blend plus the other sounds.

2. Look at the word.
- Study the sequence of letters. Note the letters that spell the sounds.
- Train yourself to see the word as the blend plus the other letters.

3. Think about the word.
- Think about how it sounds.
- Think about how it looks.
- Think about the word as the blend plus the other letters.

4. Write the word.
- Ask yourself, "Does the word look right?"
- Check the spelling of the word.
- Write the word again if you are not sure of the spelling.

Day 2 in Detail

1. Review the Sight Words

Give an ungraded practice quiz on all the sight words in the lesson. Use the same procedure as you did for the pretest—saying the word, using it in a sentence, and saying it again. Students do not need to skip three lines between words this time.

Have students correct the quiz by checking their spelling against the sight word list. You should take a quick look at their quizzes, since poor spellers often do not catch all their misspelled words.

If students need additional help learning the sight words, give them a drill exercise such as one of the following:

- Have students copy the words they misspelled.
- Have them copy short phrases or sentences which include words they misspelled. You will need to make these up ahead of time.
- Have them make up and write short phrases or sentences containing the words they missed.

2. Review the Listening Exercise

Go over the listening exercise again. Continue to emphasize the blend in each word in the word lists. Although this may seem tedious, it is essential in order to develop in students a sense of the structure and pattern of language, which then permits them to systematically analyze the spelling of words.

3. Introduce the Other Material Presented in the Lesson

Each lesson also includes work in such areas as adding endings, dictionary work, homonyms, and writing activities. Introduce this material and have students complete the corresponding exercises either in class or for homework. The lesson notes explain how to present these exercises.

4. Assign Homework

Have students prepare for graded quizzes on the sight words and the representative words. Also have students review any new material you introduced today. They should complete exercises related to the new material if they did not do those exercises during class.

Day 3 in Detail

1. Review the Listening Exercise

Go over the listening exercise again. Continue to emphasize the blend in each word in the word lists.

2. Review the Other Material Presented in the Lesson

Review any other material presented in the lesson and go over any exercises done for homework. If students have had trouble with the material either in the exercises or the dictation sentences, you may need to develop additional exercises to reinforce it.

3. Complete the Writing Sentences Exercise

You will need to dictate the sentences in this exercise. These sentences include sight words, representative words, and other material from the current lesson.

You may need to dictate the longer sentences twice. Encourage students to listen to the entire sentence and repeat it to themselves before they begin to write. This strategy will help students to develop their skill in remembering what they hear—an important skill for success in both academic and everyday situations.

After students have written the sentences, have them pair up and compare their sentences. At the same time, you should also quickly check their sentences. Pay particular attention to the spelling of the sight words and representative words and their ability to apply the other material presented in the lesson.

4. Give Spelling Quizzes

Give two graded spelling quizzes. One quiz should contain all the sight words. The other quiz should consist of representative words containing the blends introduced in the lesson. In general, we recommend that you select 10 to 15 words for this quiz. Use your own judgment about which words to select. If your students are having trouble with spelling, you may want to include only one-syllable words and avoid the more difficult vowel spellings. If your students are doing quite well, you might include the words of two or more syllables, or you might include words that contain the blends but were not listed in the listening exercise. Use the usual procedure for dictating words.

You should correct these quizzes. Students should have mastered these words by this time and should not misspell more than one word on each quiz.

Have students keep two separate personal spelling lists in their notebooks. One list should contain sight words they misspell on their quizzes. The other list should contain representative words they misspell. When students misspell a word on a quiz, have them add the word to the appropriate list. Have students copy their lists once a day, saying each word as they write it.

Give students the opportunity to take spelling quizzes on their personal spelling lists periodically. They can check off words on their lists when they have mastered them. This will give them a sense of accomplishment.

How to Use the Unit and Book Reviews

Reviews for each unit and for each book provide additional reviews of sight words, representative words, and skills that have been presented and reinforced in the lessons. Suggested words for unit and book spelling tests are included in the notes for each review.

We suggest that you use two class sessions to complete each review. Divide the work into manageable units. You will probably want students to complete some exercises in class with your assistance. You may decide to preview other exercises in class and have students complete them as part of their homework. Also as part of their homework, students should review the sight words and representative words in preparation for the unit spelling tests. They should pay particular attention to words on their personal spelling lists.

Suggested word lists for both representative and sight words are included in the notes for each review. However, you may want to adapt these tests to emphasize words your students are having particular trouble with. Correctly spelling 90 percent of the words on each test should be considered mastery. Have students check off any words on their personal spelling lists which they have now mastered. Also have them add any misspelled words to the appropriate list.

Adapting the Lesson Format

This series can be successfully used in tutorial, small group, and large group settings. The recommended lesson format was designed to be used with a small group of students who are all working on the same lesson. If you are tutoring a single student, or if your students are working on different levels, you may want to revise the recommended format to meet the needs of your special situation. The suggestions which follow are intended to help you make the best use of this series.

Tutoring a Single Student

The word patterns approach to spelling has been used successfully in a tutorial setting using the recommended lesson format. You may be able to cover the material a bit faster when working with a single student. You certainly will be able to observe a single student closely and gear the pace of the material to meet that student's needs. Avoid the temptation of helping the student so much that he or she does not have the opportunity to take full advantage of the discovery approach.

Teaching Students at Different Levels

It is possible that, based on the results of the diagnostic/placement test, students may be working in any of the four books and you may have as many as four groups to deal with. Here are some suggestions for working out ways to spend time with each group.

- Have different groups working on different parts of the lessons on any given day. For example, the Book 1 group might be working on the Day 1 material, the Book 2 group might be working on the Day 2 material, and so on. At least one group may not work on spelling at all on a given day.
- Spend the beginning of class with one group. Spend the latter part of class with another group. The groups that you are not working with directly can be working on other material.
- Audio tape the sight words pretests and practice tests, the dictation exercises, and the two spelling quizzes. This will prove to be a great timesaver for you—especially if you are dealing with several groups or if absenteeism is a problem.
- Have a reliable student who is working in one of the later spelling books give some of the quizzes and tests to students working in earlier books.

4. Other Considerations

Building Spelling Awareness

As students work through *Patterns in Spelling*, they should develop a sense of their personal spelling strengths and weaknesses. This sense should come not only from the words they are exposed to in the series but also from the words they use in their writing. Beginning spellers tend to feel that they are weak in all areas, and, indeed, it may require some time for relative strengths and weakness to show themselves. But it will become evident, for instance, that a student has more trouble spelling some vowel sounds than others.

Look for recurring patterns of strength and weakness in students' spelling. Examine their personal spelling lists and their writing. Does one student spell phonetically and thus correctly spell words that follow phonic principles but misspell those that do not? Does another student have more trouble spelling the middle of words than the beginning or end? Do errors involve specific short vowel sounds or consonant digraphs?

Help students to develop a sense of their spelling strengths. If they regularly spell representative words correctly or accurately apply the pattern for doubling the final consonant, point this out to them. You can also point out how many words they are learning to spell by having them examine the representative and sight word lists which appear at the back of each book. Also point out the many words that they are spelling correctly in their writing. As students become aware of personal spelling strengths, they begin to feel confident about their spelling and are better able to focus their learning attention on areas of weakness.

Help students to detect those areas of weakness. Students who are aware of their weaknesses can address them more directly than students who are not. Once a student is aware of a weakness, two things should be done. The student should begin to give the area of weakness extra attention and study and be encouraged to develop a healthy sense of doubt when writing words that fall into the area of weakness. If, for example, a student has difficulty applying the doubling of the final consonant pattern, lessons that deal with this should be reviewed for homework. In written work, the student should be encouraged to proofread for words that are built from roots ending with a consonant-vowel-consonant pattern. He should then check his spelling of the word against what is predicted by the pattern before checking the spelling in a dictionary.

Misspelled Words in Students' Writing

Errors in students' writing can be divided into two broad categories: those in words that students have studied and those in words that students have not yet studied. Each group can be informative.

Try to determine the source of the errors in words that have been studied. Does the evidence suggest that the student has misunderstood something, has failed to make a connection between spelling and meaning, has not studied enough, or has a poor visual memory for words he has studied?

Misspelled words that have not been studied can be handled in a variety of ways. If a student has misspelled many words in a piece of writing, pointing out all of them can discourage the student. We suggest that you again look for patterns. If you find a pattern and address it, you will be teaching the student to spell a number of words correctly rather than just one.

You might also consider pointing out high utility words—ones students are apt to use frequently. Learning to spell such words correctly will considerably cut down on the number of words misspelled.

Also consider asking students which misspelled words they most want to learn to spell. Adult learners, particularly, should have some control over what they learn.

Have your students create a third personal word list for words they misspell in their writing. You might suggest that they buy a small notebook and devote one page to each letter of the alphabet. As students enter words that are troublesome to them, they create their own personal dictionaries. They can carry these with them and easily refer to them.

Errors in words that have not been studied should not be treated negatively. Find something to praise, even if it is only the effort. Take the time to point out what was done correctly. Remember that your students may be attempting things beyond their skill level.

A Last Word

To a certain degree, success in spelling correlates to students' understanding and appreciation of the language as a whole. This series attempts to instill in students an understanding, appreciation, and enjoyment of language. But no series can hope to be responsive to all the questions students have. You can greatly enhance the learning experience by encouraging questions about the language and correlating what the student is learning in spelling to what the student is learning in reading or other areas of study.

Scope and Sequence: Book 3

Blends and Digraphs — Lesson	1	2	3	4	5	R1	6	7	8	R2	9	10	R3	11	12	R4	13	14	15	16	17	18	R5	19	20	21	R6	BR
Learn words containing consonant blends, digraphs, or silent consonants:																												
1. Two-letter initial blends	●	●	●	●	●	●																						●
2. Digraphs and suffixes							●	●	●	●																		●
3. Three-letter initial blends											●	●	●															●
4. Ending blends														●	●	●	●	●	●	●	●	●	●					●
5. Silent consonants																								●	●	●	●	●
Word Study — Lesson	**1**	**2**	**3**	**4**	**5**	**R1**	**6**	**7**	**8**	**R2**	**9**	**10**	**R3**	**11**	**12**	**R4**	**13**	**14**	**15**	**16**	**17**	**18**	**R5**	**19**	**20**	**21**	**R6**	**BR**
1. Spell sight words	●	●	●	●	●	●	●	●	●	●	●	●	●	●	●	●	●	●	●	●	●	●	●	●	●	●	●	●
2. Learn/review spelling patterns:																												
VCe words	●																											
One-syllable words ending in *ff*, *ll*, or *ss*	●																											
/k/ spelled *ck*	●																											
/ch/ spelled *tch*	●																											
Doubling Pattern 1		●		●							●																	●
Doubling Pattern 2			●	●							●			●														●
The soft *c*					●																							
Predicting the spelling of /shən/		●					●			●													●					●
Silent *e* Pattern 1											●			●								●						●
The ending *-es*											●																	
Changing *y* to *i*											●	●																●
Changing *f* to *v*											●								●									●
Silent *e* Pattern 2														●	●							●	●					●
Showing comparisons with *er/est*, *more/most*																	●						●					●
3. Discriminate between similar sounds		●	●						●					●	●		●											
4. Identify the accented syllable			●																									
5. Use possesive and reflexive pronouns				●		●													●									
6. Spell homonyms				●	●	●			●	●		●						●			●	●	●		●		●	●
7. Learn alternative spellings for the same sound:																												
/sk/ spelled *sc, sk*, or *sch*					●	●																						
/shən/ spelled *tion, sion*, or *cian*							●			●										●			●					●
/k/ spelled *ch*								●																				
/sh/ spelled *ch*								●																				
/chur/ spelled *ture* or *cher*								●		●																		
/ns/ spelled *nce, nse*, or *nts*														●		●												
/ld/ spelled *ld, led*, or *lled*																		●					●					
/kt/ spelled *ct* or *cked*																				●			●					

Word Study Lesson	1	2	3	4	5	R1	6	7	8	R2	9	10	R3	11	12	R4	13	14	15	16	17	18	R5	19	20	21	R6	BR
7. Learn alternative spellings (cont.):																												
/rs/ spelled *rce* or *rse*																						●	●					
/səl/ spelled *stle, sel*, or *sle*																									●			
8. Recognize that *tw* can carry the meaning *two*					●																							
9. Complete word puzzles						●		●		●		●	●		●	●		●				●	●				●	●
10. Identify silent consonants in consonant pairs and clusters																								●	●	●		
11. Develop/learn mnemonic devices																								●	●			●
12. Write words containing silent consonants																											●	
Word Structure Lesson	**1**	**2**	**3**	**4**	**5**	**R1**	**6**	**7**	**8**	**R2**	**9**	**10**	**R3**	**11**	**12**	**R4**	**13**	**14**	**15**	**16**	**17**	**18**	**R5**	**19**	**20**	**21**	**R6**	**BR**
1. Recognize/identify/categorize syllable types:																												
Closed (**CVC**)	●	●		●		●															●							
Open	●	●		●		●															●							
Cle	●	●		●		●															●							
VCe	●	●		●		●															●							
Double vowel	●	●		●		●															●							
2. Use the apostrophe to form:																												
Possessives	●		●			●		●		●								●										●
Plurals of letters and abbreviations									●	●								●										●
Contractions									●	●								●										●
3. Write words by syllables		●		●		●	●					●				●			●		●							
4. Form compound words		●													●		●	●	●	●			●			●		
5. Add endings:																												
to **CVC** words		●		●		●							●															●
to two-syllable words that end in **CVC**				●		●					●		●															●
-tion to verbs to form nouns							●													●								
to words that end in **C**y												●	●															●
-es to form plurals													●															●
to words that end in silent *e*													●	●	●	●						●	●					●
-ance or *-ence* to verbs to form nouns														●														
to words that end in *ce* or *ge*														●	●	●						●	●					●
to words that end in *lf*																			●									●
-ion to verbs to form nouns																				●								
6. Add affixes to root words				●		●	●						●	●			●			●	●							
7. Complete words by filling in missing letters and syllables			●				●	●		●	●			●		●							●				●	●

Word Structure — Lesson	1	2	3	4	5	R1	6	7	8	R2	9	10	R3	11	12	R4	13	14	15	16	17	18	R5	19	20	21	R6	BR
8. Build words using initial blends or digraphs and word families			●		●	●							●															●
9. Identify/study root words							●	●		●	●						●		●				●					●
10. Form ordinal numbers									●																			
11. Build words using ending blends and word parts																●		●					●					●
12. Form comparatives and superlatives																	●		●									●
Writing — Lesson	**1**	**2**	**3**	**4**	**5**	**R1**	**6**	**7**	**8**	**R2**	**9**	**10**	**R3**	**11**	**12**	**R4**	**13**	**14**	**15**	**16**	**17**	**18**	**R5**	**19**	**20**	**21**	**R6**	**BR**
1. Write words from dictation	●	●	●	●	●		●	●	●	●	●	●		●	●		●	●	●	●	●	●		●	●	●		
2. Write sentences from dictation	●	●	●	●	●	●	●	●	●	●	●	●	●	●	●	●	●	●	●	●	●	●	●	●	●	●	●	
3. Compose sentences		●		●	●	●	●	●		●	●	●	●	●	●	●	●	●	●	●	●	●	●	●	●		●	●
4. Complete sentences			●	●	●	●			●				●					●	●		●	●				●		●
5. Write phrases from dictation						●						●				●	●	●					●					
6. Compose paragraphs						●							●			●				●								
7. Compose a letter									●																			
8. Complete cloze exercises																										●		
9. Compose a story																										●		
Dictionary Skills — Lesson	**1**	**2**	**3**	**4**	**5**	**R1**	**6**	**7**	**8**	**R2**	**9**	**10**	**R3**	**11**	**12**	**R4**	**13**	**14**	**15**	**16**	**17**	**18**	**R5**	**19**	**20**	**21**	**R6**	**BR**
1. Alphabetize words	●																											
2. Determine compound word spellings		●																	●	●			●			●		
3. Select from alternative spellings					●			●						●						●		●			●			
4. Learn the meaning of words					●			●			●						●					●		●	●			
5. Determine homonym spellings					●													●			●				●	●		
6. Confirm correct spellings							●		●	●	●								●	●								
7. Find the origins of words								●																				
8. Use the guide words												●																
9. Learn/use the related words strategy for silent consonants																								●	●		●	●

Lesson 1

The Blends *bl*, *cl*, *fl*, *gl*, and *pl*

Objectives

- **Blends:** Learn to spell words with the blends *bl*, *cl*, *fl*, *gl*, and *pl*.
- **Sight Words:** Learn to spell *million*, *billion*, *iron*, *house*, *America*, and *century*.
- **Dictionary Skills:** Review alphabetizing words by the first three, four, or five letters.
- **One-Syllable Word Patterns:** Identify representative words that follow patterns studied in Books 1 and 2: **VCe** and short vowel words that end in *ff*, *ll*, *ss*, *ck*, and *tch*.
- **Syllable Types:** Review the attributes of closed, open, **Cle**, **VCe**, and double vowel syllables and write an example of each.
- **Cle Syllables:** Write dictated words that end with **Cle** syllables.
- **Possessives:** Learn a three-step process for forming possessives.
- **Writing Sentences:** Practice writing representative and sight words in context.

Lesson 1

The Blends *bl*, *cl*, *fl*, *gl*, and *pl*

Sight Words		
million	iron	America
billion	house	century

Blends

1 Listening

bl

Listen to the sound of *bl* in these words.

black	blend	blame	blue
bless	blank	blaze	blow
bluff	blanket	blotch	blown

cl

Listen to the sound of *cl* in these words.

clap	class	claim
clip	clock	clean
cliff	clutch	clear

fl

Listen to the sound of *fl* in these words.

flag	fling	flame	fly
flat	flock	flare	flee
fled	fluid	flight	fleet

gl

Listen to the sound of *gl* in these words.

glad	glow	glare
glass	glue	gleam
glove	glum	glide

pl

Listen to the sound of *pl* in these words.

plan	place	explain	reply
pledge	plane	complain	employ
plenty	please	complete	explore

4 Lesson 1

Sight Words

Teach the sight words using the methods described on pages 9-12 in the introduction to this book.

1 Listening

Explain to students that blends are a combination of two or three consonants in which each consonant can still be heard. When students are producing the sound that the blends make, be sure that they are saying /bl/, not /bul/. They must understand that there is no vowel sound present in a blend.

Introduce the words with the blend *bl* using the following method.

T: Look at the first group of words. These words all have the blend *bl*. Listen to the sound of *bl*. (Say /bl/.) What letters make the sound /bl/?
S: *B-l*.
T: Good. What sound do the letters *b-l* make?
S: /bl/.
T: Good. Listen to the sound of /bl/ in the word *black*. (Say *black*.) Now listen again. (Say *black* again.) What letters make the sound /bl/?
S: *B-l*.
T: Good. What letters make the /ak/ sound in *black*?
S: *A-c-k*.
T: Good. What letters spell *black*?
S: *B-l-a-c-k*.
T: Now look at the second word. Listen to the sound of /bl/ in the word *bless*. (Say *bless*). What letters make the sound /bl/?
S: *B-l*.
T: Good. What letters make the /es/ sound in *bless*?
S: *E-s-s*.
T: Good. What letters spell *bless*?
S: *B-l-e-s-s*.
T: What does *b-l-e-s-s* spell?
S: *Bless*.
T: What does *b-l-a-c-k* spell?
S: *Black*.
T: Good.

2 Writing Words. On the lines below, write the words that you hear.

1. flock	4. blotch	7. please
2. clean	5. complain	8. blow
3. glass	6. flame	9. clear

3 Dictionary Skills: Alphabetizing. On the lines below, alphabetize the words in Exercise 2.

1. blotch	4. clear	7. flock
2. blow	5. complain	8. glass
3. clean	6. flame	9. please

4 Review of One-Syllable Word Patterns. Review the following patterns that were covered in Books 1 and 2 of this series. On the lines provided, write words from Exercise 1 that are examples of each pattern.

Pattern: A one-syllable word with a long vowel sound often ends in silent *e*.

1. blame	3. flame	5. glide
2. blaze	4. flare	6. please

Pattern: When one-syllable words with a short vowel end with the sounds /f/, /l/, or /s/, the final sound is usually spelled *ff*, *ll*, or *ss*.

1. bless	3. cliff	5. glass
2. bluff	4. class	

Pattern: The letters *ck* are usually used to spell the sound /k/ at the end of a one-syllable word with a short vowel.

1. black	2. clock	3. flock

Pattern: The letters *tch* are usually used to spell the sound /ch/ at the end of a one-syllable word with a short vowel.

1. blotch	2. clutch

Lesson 1 5

Read the rest of the representative words containing *bl* one column at a time. Then have the students read and spell the words with you.

Follow the same steps to introduce the words with the blends *cl*, *fl*, *gl*, and *pl*.

1. Say the sound /cl/ and ask students what letters make the sound.
2. Say the letters *c-l* and ask students what sound they make.
3. Say the word *clap* and ask students what letters spell /cl/ and what letters spell /ap/.
4. Say the word *clap* and ask students what letters spell *clap*.

When working on a specific word, review any pattern that students have already learned, such as the double *f* at the end of *bluff* or the *ame* at the end of *blame*. Exercise 4 reviews some of these patterns also.

Point out that *glove* is an unusual spelling because the silent *e* does not produce a long vowel. Remind them of the sight word *love*, which they studied in Book 1 of this series.

After you have completed the last list of representative words, read aloud the words in the lists again. Ask students to identify the words which contain two or more syllables as you are reading. Refer to the introduction to Book 1 if students need more practice hearing syllables.

Make sure students understand the meanings of all the representative words before going on with the lesson.

2 Writing Words

Instruct students to write the words that you dictate, which are found on the replica of the student page. Say each word, use it in a phrase or simple sentence, and say the word again.

3 Dictionary Skills: Alphabetizing

Before introducing this exercise, be sure your students know the sequence of the alphabet and which letters are vowels. You may want students to write the alphabet on an index card or piece of paper and tape it to the inside cover of their books.

This exercise reviews alphabetizing words by the first three, four, or five letters. Book 1 of this series has many exercises which help students to develop this skill. If a student is having trouble alphabetizing, follow the suggestions in the introduction to Book 1.

4 Review of One-Syllable Word Patterns

This exercise reviews word families studied in Books 1 and 2 of this series. The **VCe** pattern was introduced in Book 2, and the other three patterns were covered in Book 1.

The answers on the replica of the student page are examples. Accept all correct responses.

5 Review of Syllable Types. In Book 2 of this series, you learned to identify five types of syllables. Review these syllable types and write one example of each type on the lines below.

1. A **closed** syllable ends with a short vowel followed by one or more consonants.
2. An **open** syllable ends with a vowel that is usually long.
3. A **Cle** syllable has a consonant plus *le* and usually comes at the end of a word.
4. A **VCe** syllable has a long vowel followed by a consonant and ends in a silent *e*.
5. A **double vowel** syllable has two vowels together that make one sound.

Syllable Type	Example	Your Example
1. Closed	set	______
2. Open	re	______
3. Cle	ble	______
4. VCe	ake	______
5. Double Vowel	eem	______

6 Writing Words with Cle Syllables. The consonant pairs in Exercise 1 of this lesson are often used in Cle syllables. When *bl, cl, fl, gl,* and *pl* are used to form Cle syllables, they are not pronounced as blends. For example, *ble* is pronounced /bŭl/ or /bəl/. Write the words you hear, which all end in Cle syllables.

1. double	4. raffle	7. uncle
2. single	5. people	8. example
3. couple	6. trouble	9. muffle

6 Lesson 1

5 Review of Syllable Types

This exercise reviews the five types of syllables that were studied in Book 2 of this series. Review the attributes of each syllable type before students write their own examples.

Note any syllable types with which students have difficulty.

6 Writing Words with Cle Syllables

The consonant pairs in this lesson are often found in Cle syllables. Emphasize to students that the pronunciation of the consonant pair changes from that of a blend to that of a Cle syllable. Contrast the pronunciation of the blend /bl/ with the pronunciation of the Cle syllable /bul/. Make sure students can hear the difference. Then dictate the words that are found on the replica of the student page.

7 The Possessive Apostrophe. When something belongs to someone or something, use an apostrophe (') to show ownership or possession. Follow the steps below.

Step 1: Write the owner(s) or possessor(s).

a boy	the clocks
the class	the children

Step 2: Add an apostrophe.

a boy'	the clocks'
the class'	the children'

Step 3: Add an *s* if you can hear one when you say the phrase.

a boy's best friend	the clocks' hands
the class's field trips	the children's playground

Rewrite the phrases below to show possession.

1. the wings of the airplanes — the airplanes' wings
2. the bicycle of Uncle John — Uncle John's bicycle
3. the leaves of the trees — the trees' leaves
4. the clothes of Chris — Chris's clothes
5. the color of the glass — the glass's color
6. the choice of the people — the people's choice

8 Writing Sentences. On the lines below, write the sentences that you hear.

1. Did Jeff explain how to get to Jack's house?
2. The fluid made a black blotch on Clara's glove.
3. Please clean the kitchen and iron the clothes today.
4. By 1750, more than a million people lived in America.
5. We need one billion in pledges by the end of the century.

Lesson 1 7

7 The Possessive Apostrophe

This book will introduce and review various uses of the apostrophe. The *'s* used to show possession was introduced in Book 1. Remind students that people and things can possess other things, and model a few simple phrases or ask for some oral examples.

The three-step process introduced in this exercise can be used in forming all written possessives, whether the possessor is singular or plural and whether or not it ends in *s*. This approach is based on the fact that students generally form oral possessives correctly, i.e., they don't say *clocks's* (/kloksez/).

When students have rewritten the phrases using apostrophes, have them read the phrases aloud. If they have added *'s* to any plural nouns ending in *s* (the only form that does not add *'s*), have them say these words aloud so they can see that this is not the way these possessives are pronounced.

8 Writing Sentences

Instruct students to write the sentences you dictate, which are on the replica of the student page. For the first few lessons, you may need to read some sentences twice. Encourage students to listen to the entire sentence and repeat it to themselves before they begin to write. This strategy will help them to develop their auditory memories.

These sentences give students an opportunity to write the sight words and some of the representative words in context. Note any specific errors that students make, and design additional words, sentences, or phrases for specific problems.

Sentence 1 is a question. You may want to review the use of the question mark before you begin.

In addition to the blends covered in this lesson, the patterns found in these sentences include:
— possessives (1 and 2)
— Silent *e* Pattern 1 (4)

Lesson 2

The Blends *br*, *cr*, *fr*, and *gr*

Objectives

- **Blends:** Learn to spell words with the blends *br*, *cr*, *fr*, and *gr*.
- **Sight Words:** Learn to spell *bruise*, *cruise*, *suit*, *fruit*, *build*, and *juice*.
- **Syllable Types**: Review five types of syllables by categorizing examples.
- **Writing by Syllables:** Write dictated words one syllable at a time.
- **Sound Discrimination:** Discriminate between pairs of syllables that begin with *cr* and *gr*.
- **Difficult Words with *r* Blends:** Practice writing *library*, *February*, and *breakfast* and use them in original sentences.
- **Compound Words:** Form compound words given both elements and given only one element.
- **Pattern:** Review Doubling Pattern 1.
- **Writing Sentences:** Practice writing representative and sight words in context.

Sight Words

Teach the sight words using the methods described on pages 9-12 in the introduction to this book. All of these words have the vowel pattern *ui*. These words are presented as sight words because this vowel combination is used infrequently.

Emphasize the change in the pronunciation of *ui* in the word *build*. Point out that three of the words use blends which are studied in this lesson.

Lesson 2

The Blends *br*, *cr*, *fr*, and *gr*

Sight Words		
bruise	suit	build
cruise	fruit	juice

Blends
br
cr
fr
gr

1 Listening

Listen to the sound of *br* in these words.

brick	braid	brave	library
bridge	brain	broke	February
brush	brake	broken	breakfast

Listen to the sound of *cr* in these words.

crop	crack	crazy	cry
cross	cradle	cream	creep
crossing	crankcase	creek	crayon

Listen to the sound of *fr* in these words.

free	frog	frame	Friday
freeze	frost	afraid	France
froze	friend	fright	San Francisco

Listen to the sound of *gr* in these words.

grab	grade	agree	grapes
grand	grain	green	grease
grill	grave	greet	griddle

2 Writing Words. On the lines below, write the words that you hear.

1. France
2. grill
3. cradle
4. brush
5. cream
6. friend
7. agree
8. bridge
9. afraid

8 Lesson 2

1 Listening

Introduce the words with the blend *br* using the following steps.

1. Say the sound /br/ and ask students what letters make the sound.
2. Say the letters *b-r* and ask students what sound they make.
3. Say the word *brick* and ask students what letters spell /br/ and what letters spell /ik/.
4. Say the word *brick* and ask students what letters spell *brick*.

Follow the same steps to introduce the words with the blends *cr*, *fr*, and *gr*.

When students are producing the sounds that the blends make, be sure that they are saying /br/, not /bur/. Reinforce the idea that there is no vowel sound present in a blend.

When working on a specific word, review any pattern that students have already learned, such as *dge* to spell /j/ at the end of *bridge*, the double *s* at the end of *cross*, and *ain* to spell /an/ at the end of *brain* and *grain*.

Most of the representative words contain word families that students have studied in Books 1 and 2 of this series. Some of the words,

3 Review of Syllable Types. Write each syllable below on a line under the correct heading. The first one has been done to get you started.

√froze	cra	green	braid	ble
grab	brake	bri	gle	cross
fro	ple	frame	grease	brick

	Closed	Open	Cle
1.	grab	fro	ple
2.	cross	cra	gle
3.	brick	bri	ble

	VCe	Double Vowel
1.	froze	green
2.	brake	braid
3.	frame	grease

4 Writing Words by Syllables. Write each word your teacher dictates by syllables. Then write the whole word on the line provided.

	First Syllable	Second Syllable	Third Syllable	Fourth Syllable	Whole Word
1.	ex	plain			explain
2.	cray	on			crayon
3.	un	friend	ly		unfriendly
4.	um	brell	a		umbrella
5.	a	gree	a	ble	agreeable
6.	in	creas	ing	ly	increasingly

Lesson 2 9

however, contain other vowel spellings which will be dealt with in Book 4. You do not need to hold students responsible for all of these representative words.

You may want to concentrate on helping students learn the more common and useful words with unusual vowel combinations, such as *friend*. Point out the silent *i* in *friend* and suggest that it be treated like a sight word by any student who has particular trouble learning how to spell it.

Make sure students know the meanings of all the representative words before going on with the lesson.

2 Writing Words

Instruct students to write the words that you dictate, which are found on the replica of the student page. Say each word, use it in a phrase or simple sentence, and say the word again.

3 Review of Syllable Types

Review the attributes of each syllable type before students begin this exercise. Be sure they understand that they are to categorize the syllables by writing them on the lines under the appropriate headings.

4 Writing Words by Syllables

This type of exercise was introduced in Book 1. The strategy of writing longer words syllable by syllable can give students more confidence in predicting the spelling of words they haven't studied and help to make them more independent spellers.

Before beginning the dictation, point out that the number of blanks for each word indicates the number of syllables in that particular word.

Dictate the words on the replica of the student page by syllables, emphasizing the syllables. Have students write the syllables in the short blanks. Then pronounce the whole word normally, and have students write it on the line provided.

When all the words have been dictated, have students identify each syllable by type.

Don't worry about formal syllable divisions. Emphasize the division students hear. It is more important for them to spell the word correctly than to have their syllabication match that of the dictionary.

Additional Exercise:

Have students use two or three of these words in sentences.

❺ Distinguishing Between *cr* and *gr*

It is difficult for some students to discriminate between the /k/ and /g/ sounds. This exercise is designed to help you identify students who have this difficulty. Dictate the following syllables, instructing students to underline the one they hear in each pair found on the student page.

1. crid	6. grim
2. crel	7. crep
3. gron	8. grot
4. crub	9. cruz
5. grad	10. craf

If students have difficulty with this exercise, it will be necessary to spend some time helping them to hear the differences in these sounds. Try the following strategies.

1. Dictate the syllables and ask students to spell them.
2. Ask students to read the list of syllables to you, listening carefully to their pronunciation. Model the correct sounds for them.
3. Make up other syllable pairs for continued practice, if necessary.

❻ Using Words with *r* Blends

This exercise focuses on three words that students often find difficult to spell. *Library* is frequently mispronounced and therefore misspelled by students. Have students emphasize the *r* in the *br* blend when pronouncing *library*. /Fĕb′ yo͞o ĕ rē/ is accepted as a second pronunciation for *February* and is very common. However, if students have trouble remembering the first *r*, have them emphasize it when pronouncing *February*, also.

Point out that *breakfast* literally means "to break fast." Knowing this can help students to remember how to spell this word.

❺ Distinguishing Between *cr* and *gr*. Underline the syllable you hear.

1. crid — grid	5. crad — grad	9. cruz — gruz
2. crel — grel	6. crim — grim	10. craf — graf
3. cron — gron	7. crep — grep	
4. crub — grub	8. crot — grot	

❻ Using Words with *r* Blends. On the lines below, write the words that you hear.

1. library 2. February 3. breakfast

Use each of these words in sentences of your own.

1. ______
2. ______
3. ______

❼ Word Building: Compound Words. Form the compound words indicated below. All of these compounds are closed.

1. grape + fruit	grapefruit	5. brain + storm	brainstorm
2. friend + ship	friendship	6. frost + bite	frostbite
3. draw + bridge	drawbridge	7. out + cry	outcry
4. grand + mother	grandmother	8. griddle + cake	griddlecake

Write three compound words formed with each of the words below. The given words can be at either the beginning or the end of the compound words, for example, *greenhouse* and *evergreen*. Use your dictionary to see if your compounds are closed, hyphenated, or open.

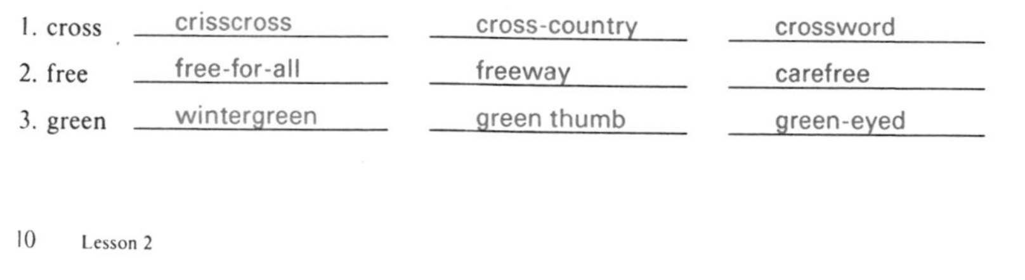

1. cross	crisscross	cross-country	crossword
2. free	free-for-all	freeway	carefree
3. green	wintergreen	green thumb	green-eyed

10 Lesson 2

❼ Word Building: Compound Words

Remind students that compound words are made by combining two words and that this is one way words are formed in English. Generally, no letters are added or dropped when compound words are formed.

After students write the designated compound words in the first part of this exercise, they are asked to write nine compound words of their own.

Review the three ways compound words can be written. Remind students that dictionaries do not always agree on whether a compound should be closed, hyphenated, or open.

You might also want to mention that sometimes a compound used as an adjective will be closed or hyphenated, while it will be an open compound when used as a noun, for example, *freehand* (adjective) and *free hand* (noun).

Explain to students that sometimes a compound word will be listed at the end of the entry for the first word, rather than as a separate entry.

8 Doubling Pattern 1. Review Doubling Pattern 1, which was introduced in Book 1 of this series, and follow the directions below.

Pattern: Double the final consonant if a word has one syllable, one vowel, and one final consonant, and the ending begins with a vowel. Do not double *w* or *x*.

1. Look at each word below. If the word has one syllable, one vowel, or one final consonant, check the appropriate box. If you check all three boxes and the ending begins with a vowel, double the final consonant before adding the ending. Do not double *w* or *x*.
2. If you do not check all three boxes or the ending begins with a consonant, do not double the final consonant. Write the word on the line provided.

	One syllable	One vowel	One final consonant		
1. grill	✓	✓		+ ed	grilled
2. grab	✓	✓	✓	+ ing	grabbing
3. brag	✓	✓	✓	+ ed	bragged
4. free	✓			+ dom	freedom
5. flood	✓		✓	+ ed	flooded
6. brush	✓	✓		+ ing	brushing
7. flex	✓	✓	✓	+ ible	flexible
8. grin	✓	✓	✓	+ ing	grinning

9 Writing Sentences. On the lines below, write the sentences that you hear.

1. Are you getting that blue suit for the cruise?
2. The creek froze on Friday, and we could walk across it.
3. Grace had fruit juice and griddlecakes for breakfast.
4. We are planning to build a brick house on Bridge Street.
5. Bill got a bruise when his friend tripped him by mistake.

Lesson 2 11

8 Doubling Pattern 1

This is a review of the doubling pattern that students studied in Book 1. Be sure students understand the doubling pattern before doing the exercise. You might do the first one or two items together as a group.

If students need further practice with doubling, give them more words to practice with. This part of the doubling rule must be firmly in place because the remaining lessons in this unit will address doubling the final consonant in words of two or more syllables.

9 Writing Sentences

Instruct students to write the sentences you dictate, which are on the replica of the student page. For the first few lessons, you may need to read some sentences twice. Encourage students to listen to the entire sentence and repeat it to themselves before they begin to write. This strategy will help them to develop their auditory memories.

These sentences give students an opportunity to write the sight words and some of the representative words in context. Note any specific errors that students make, and design additional words, sentences, or phrases for specific problems.

Students should remember to start each sentence with a capital letter and end it with a period or question mark. You may want to discuss the use of commas when they are called for in the sentences. Use your own judgment on this.

In addition to the blends covered in this lesson, the patterns found in these sentences include:
—Doubling Pattern 1 (1, 4, and 5)
—compound words (3)

Lesson 3

The Blends *pr*, *tr*, and *dr*

Sight Words		
salad	chocolate	food
onion	spaghetti	refrigerator

Blends

1 Listening

pr

Listen to the sound of *pr* in these words.

pray	pretty	price	April
praise	problem	pride	improve
preach	present	prize	practice
program	president	surprise	preparing

tr

Listen to the sound of *tr* in these words.

trap	track	train	pantry
trip	trick	treat	country
trim	truck	truly	entrance
tree	trade	travel	tragedy

dr

Listen to the sound of *dr* in these words.

drag	drop	dry	dream
drug	dress	drive	hundred
drum	address	drove	children

2 Writing Words. On the lines below, write the words that you hear.

1. track	5. prize	9. improve
2. drop	6. pantry	10. travel
3. preach	7. address	11. president
4. dry	8. truly	12. practice

12 Lesson 3

Lesson 3

The Blends *pr*, *tr*, and *dr*

Objectives

- **Blends:** Learn to spell words with the blends *pr*, *tr*, and *dr*.
- **Sight Words:** Learn to spell *salad*, *onion*, *chocolate*, *spaghetti*, *food*, and *refrigerator*. Use the sight words to complete sentences.
- **Word Building:** Write the missing syllables of dictated words. Add initial blends to short- and long-vowel word families.
- **Sound Discrimination:** Discriminate between pairs of syllables containing *r* and *l* blends.
- **Possessives:** Form possessives following a three-step process.
- **Hearing Accent:** Mark the accented syllable of words that have more than one syllable.
- **Pattern:** Discover Doubling Pattern 2.
- **Writing Sentences:** Practice writing representative and sight words in context.

Sight Words

Teach the sight words using the methods described on pages 9-12 in the introduction to this book.

All of these words except *food* contain a schwa. Draw attention to the letters used for the schwa in these words, i.e., *a* in /săl əd/ and /spə gĕt ē/, *o* in /ŏn yən/ and /chŏk ə lĭt/, and *e* and *o* in /rĭ frĭj ə rā tər/. If students have particular trouble with any of these words, help them to develop mnemonics for remembering which letter to use to spell the schwa.

1 Listening

Introduce the words with the blend *pr* using the following steps.

1. Say the sound /pr/ and ask students what letters make the sound.
2. Say the letters *p-r* and ask students what sound they make.
3. Say the word *pray* and ask students what letters spell /pr/ and what letters spell /ā/.
4. Say the word *pray* and ask students what letters spell *pray*.

Follow the same steps to introduce the words with the blends *tr* and *dr*. Emphasize any patterns students have already learned, such as *each* to spell /ēch/ at the end of *preach* or *ck* to spell /k/ at the end of *track*, *trick*, and *truck*.

Point out the pronounciation of *ove* in *improve* and ask students if they remember any other words that have the same pronounciation for *ove* (*move* and *prove* were sight words in Book 2 of this series).

Make sure students know the meanings of all the representative words before going on with the lesson.

Additional Activity:

If you have students who need practice with segmentation skills, have them count the number of syllables they hear in the two- and three-syllable representative words.

3 Word Building. Write the missing syllable of each word you hear.

1. pro blem
2. sur prise
3. pro gram
4. en trance
5. pres ent
6. hun dred
7. chil dren
8. trag e dy
9. coun try

4 Using Sight Words. Fill in each blank with one of the sight words from this lesson. Use each word only once.

1. Is the chocolate milk in the refrigerator?
2. Priscilla chopped up an onion and put it in the salad.
3. I love Italian food. Pizza and spaghetti are my favorites.

5 Distinguishing Between *r* and *l*. Underline the syllable you hear.

1. brun — blun
2. grip — glip
3. frim — flim
4. crup — clup
5. prif — plif
6. brog — blog
7. grat — glat
8. fred — fled
9. crus — clus

Now write *r* or *l* in the blanks below to complete the syllable you hear.

1. b l ut
2. g r an
3. f l ub
4. c l ick
5. p r og
6. b r ib
7. g l ot
8. f r em
9. c r ad

6 Word Building with Blends Containing *r* and *l*. Write one of the *r* or *l* blends below in each blank to form a word. Do not make the same word twice.

bl gl fl cl pl br gr fr cr pr dr tr

1. bl and
2. gl and
3. tr ain
4. dr eam
5. fl ed
6. fr ee
7. pr ide
8. br ight
9. pl ight
10. cl ock
11. cr ock
12. gr ove

Lesson 3 13

2 Writing Words

Instruct students to write the words that you dictate, which are found on the replica of the student page. Say each word, use it in a phrase or simple sentence, and say the word again.

3 Word Building

In this exercise, students direct their attention to writing a single syllable of each word. This will help them to hear words by syllables and spell by syllables when they need to do so.

Dictate the entire word without emphasizing the syllabication.

Allow time for students to isolate the missing syllable and write it in the blank.

Additional Activity:

Have students identify the types of syllables that they have written.

4 Using Sight Words

This exercise gives students additional practice in writing the sight words from this lesson by using them to complete sentences.

5 Distinguishing Between *r* and *l*

It is difficult for some students to discriminate between the /r/ and /l/ sounds. This exercise is designed to help you identify students who have this difficulty.

Dictate the following syllables, instructing students to underline the one they hear in each pair found on the student page.

1. brun
2. grip
3. flim
4. crup
5. plif
6. blog
7. glat
8. fred
9. clus

Now dictate the following syllables, instructing students to fill in each blank with either *r* or *l*.

1. blut
2. gran
3. flub
4. click
5. prog
6. brib
7. glot
8. frem
9. crad

If students have difficulty with this exercise, it will be necessary to spend some time with them individually, helping them to hear the differences in these sounds. The notes for Exercise 5 in Lesson 2 contain suggestions for strategies to use.

6 Word Building with Blends Containing *r* and *l*

In this exercise, students create words by adding blends to some of the word families from Books 1 and 2. Instruct students to try each blend with each of the word families to determine which ones form words. When the blend plus the word family makes a word, they should write the blend in the blank. Encourage them to use all of the blends at least once. The answers given on the replica of the student page are examples. Many other correct responses are possible. Accept all correctly spelled words.

7 The Possessive Apostrophe

This exercise reviews the three steps to forming the possessive introduced in Lesson 1.

If students are having trouble forming the possessive, do the first one or two items with them. Have them say the phrase first (the Brents' address) and then identify the possessor (the Brents). Have them write *the Brents.* Then have them add an apostrophe. Finally, they will determine that no *s* is added because they don't hear two *s*'s.

In the second example, they will say "the story's point." They will write *story*, add an apostrophe, and then add an *s* to form *story's.* Encourage students to finish the exercise on their own.

7 The Possessive Apostrophe. Rewrite the phrases below following these steps.

Step 1: Write the owner(s) or possessor(s).

the president	the men
the nurse	several cars

Step 2: Add an apostrophe.

the president'	the men'
the nurse'	several cars'

Step 3: Add an *s* if you can hear one when you say the phrase.

the president's speech	the men's plans
the nurse's duties	several cars' fenders

1. the address of the Brents — the Brents' address
2. the point of the story — the story's point
3. the uniforms of the players — the players' uniforms
4. the sponsors of the programs — the programs' sponsors
5. the orders of the boss — the boss's orders
6. the parents of the children — the children's parents
7. the crew of the ship — the ship's crew
8. the problems of Grace — Grace's problems

8 Hearing Accent. When words of more than one syllable are pronounced, usually one syllable receives more stress than the others. We call the syllable that receives the most stress the *accented* syllable. Dictionaries use an accent mark (ʹ) in the pronunciation guide to show which syllable is accented.

Listen to the words below, and place an accent mark on the accented syllable.

1. pro´ gram	4. gal´ lop	7. prof´ it
2. num´ ber	5. for got´	8. blan´ ket
3. oc cur´	6. pro pel´	9. ben´ e fit

14 Lesson 3

8 Hearing Accent

Doubling Pattern 2, which deals with doubling final consonants in words of two or more syllables, will be introduced in Exercise 9. Exercise 8 prepares students for this pattern, which requires them to recognize the syllable that is accented.

Read the words on the replica of the student page normally, being careful not to overemphasize the accented syllables.

Some students have great difficulty identifying accented syllables. It may be necessary to work individually with these students and to practice with many more words than are provided in this exercise. If your students are able to recognize prefixes, it is helpful for them to know that prefixes are usually not accented.

If you have students who have trouble identifying the accented syllable in words, teach them to use the dictionary to verify or determine the accented syllable. Develop exercises like this one, but instead of having students listen for the accent, have them look up the accented syllable in the dictionary or have them mark the accented syllable they hear and then verify it by checking the dictionary.

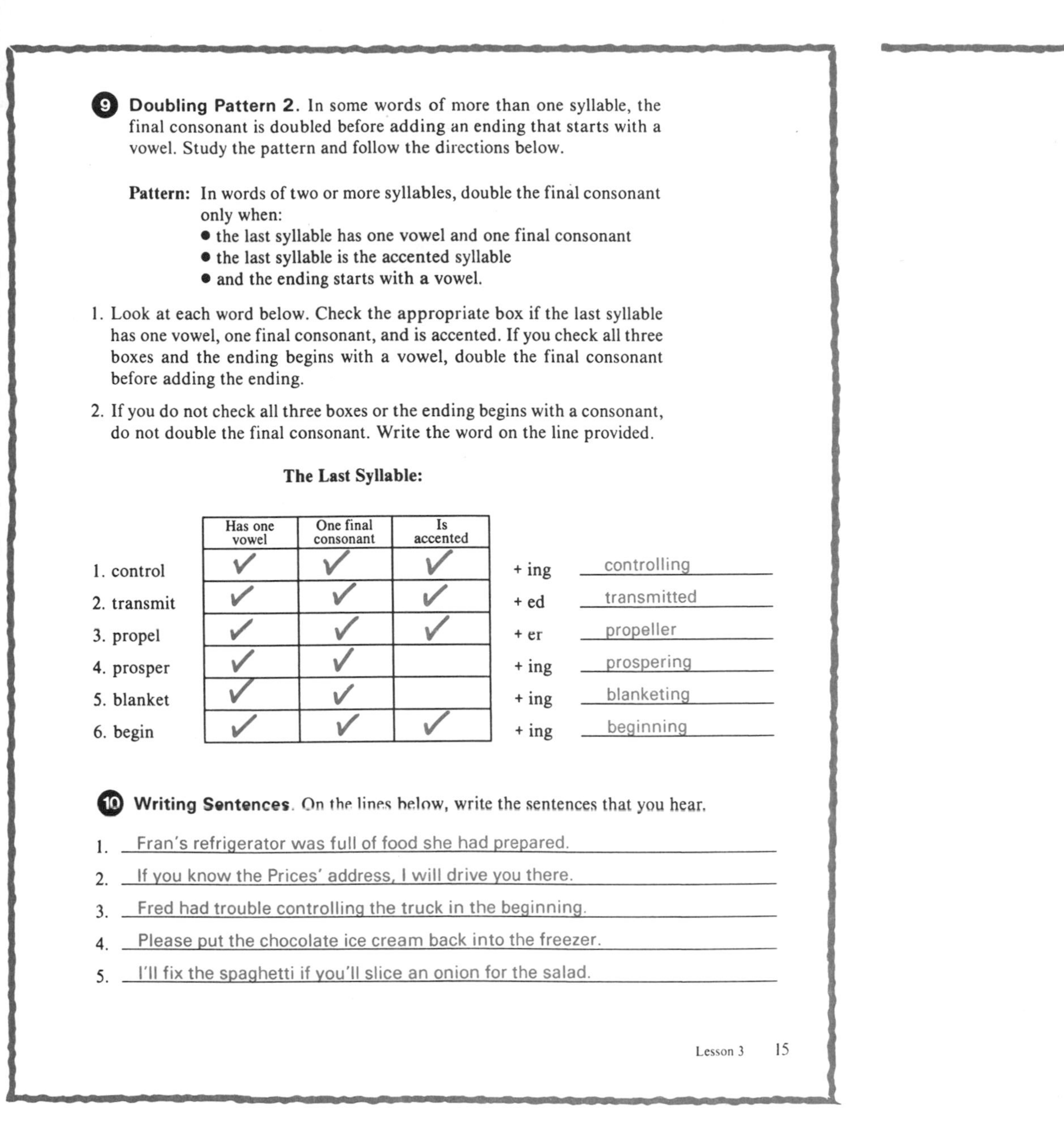

9 Doubling Pattern 2. In some words of more than one syllable, the final consonant is doubled before adding an ending that starts with a vowel. Study the pattern and follow the directions below.

Pattern: In words of two or more syllables, double the final consonant only when:
- the last syllable has one vowel and one final consonant
- the last syllable is the accented syllable
- and the ending starts with a vowel.

1. Look at each word below. Check the appropriate box if the last syllable has one vowel, one final consonant, and is accented. If you check all three boxes and the ending begins with a vowel, double the final consonant before adding the ending.
2. If you do not check all three boxes or the ending begins with a consonant, do not double the final consonant. Write the word on the line provided.

The Last Syllable:

	Has one vowel	One final consonant	Is accented		
1. control	✓	✓	✓	+ ing	controlling
2. transmit	✓	✓	✓	+ ed	transmitted
3. propel	✓	✓	✓	+ er	propeller
4. prosper	✓	✓		+ ing	prospering
5. blanket	✓	✓		+ ing	blanketing
6. begin	✓	✓	✓	+ ing	beginning

10 Writing Sentences. On the lines below, write the sentences that you hear.

1. Fran's refrigerator was full of food she had prepared.
2. If you know the Prices' address, I will drive you there.
3. Fred had trouble controlling the truck in the beginning.
4. Please put the chocolate ice cream back into the freezer.
5. I'll fix the spaghetti if you'll slice an onion for the salad.

Lesson 3 15

9 Doubling Pattern 2

Be sure students understand this doubling pattern before doing the exercise. Explain to students that this pattern is built on Doubling Pattern 1, so they already know most of the pattern. The only new part is identifying the accented syllable. You might want to do the first item together as a group.

If students need further practice doubling, give them more words to practice with. If students are not doubling correctly, take note of which aspect of the pattern they do not understand. It will quite likely be identifying the accented syllable. Have them practice identifying accented syllables in words you have selected.

10 Writing Sentences

Instruct students to write the sentences you dictate, which are on the replica of the student page. For the first few lessons, you may need to read some sentences twice. Encourage students to listen to the entire sentence and repeat it to themselves before they begin to write. This strategy will help them to develop their auditory memories.

These sentences give students an opportunity to write the sight words and some of the representative words in context. Note any specific errors that students make, and design additional words, sentences, or phrases for specific problems.

You may want to briefly review the formation of contractions before beginning to dictate these sentences.

In addition to the blends covered in this lesson, the patterns found in these sentences include:
—Silent *e* Pattern 1 (1)
—possessives (1 and 2)
—Doubling Pattern 2 (3)
—contractions (5)

Lesson 4

The Blends st, sp, sn, sl, and sm

Sight Words: certain, cereal, necessary

Blends				
st	Listen to the sound of *st* in these words.			
	stack	stay	stick	stock
	stain	stable	stiff	stuck
	stake	steam	still	study
	state	steel	stitch	stuff
sp	Listen to the sound of *sp* in these words.			
	spill	space	spice	inspect
	spell	spade	Spain	respect
	spend	speak	Spanish	special
sn	Listen to the sound of *sn* in these words.			
	snap	snail	snow	
	snack	snake	snore	
	sniff	sneak	sneeze	
sl	Listen to the sound of *sl* in these words.			
	slap	sled	slick	sleep
	slipper	slide	slice	sleeve
sm	Listen to the sound of *sm* in these words.			
	smell	smear	smile	
	small	smudge	smoke	

16 Lesson 4

Lesson 4

The Blends *st*, *sp*, *sn*, *sl*, and *sm*

Objectives

- **Blends:** Learn to spell words with the blends *st*, *sp*, *sn*, *sl*, and *sm*.
- **Sight Words:** Learn to spell *certain*, *cereal*, and *necessary*.
- **Patterns:** Add endings to words following Doubling Patterns 1 and 2.
- **Composing Sentences:** Write original sentences using selected words.
- **Writing by Syllables:** Write dictated words one syllable at a time. Identify the types of syllables in each word.
- **Possessive Pronouns:** Write dictated sentences containing possessive pronouns.
- **Homonyms:** Learn to discriminate between *its* and *it's*.
- **Writing Sentences:** Practice writing representative and sight words in context.

Sight Words

Teach the sight words using the methods described on pages 9-12 in the introduction to this book. Point out that these three sight words all spell /s/ with a *c*. The soft *c* will be discussed in Lesson 5

❶ Listening

Introduce the words with the blend *st* using the following steps.

1. Say the sound /st/ and ask students what letters make the sound.
2. Say the letters *s-t* and ask students what sound they make.
3. Say the word *stack* and ask students what letters spell /st/ and what letters spell /ak/.
4. Say the word *stack* and ask students what letters spell *stack*.

Follow the same steps to introduce the words with the blends *sp*, *sn*, *sl*, and *sm*.

Review any other patterns that students have already learned, such as *tch* to spell /ch/ at the end of *stitch*, eaC to spell long *e* in *steam*, *speak*, *sneak*, and *smear*, and *ow* to spell long *o* at the end of *snow*. Point out the *ci* spelling of /sh/ in *special*. Various other spellings of /sh/ will be covered in Lesson 6.

Make sure that students know the meanings of all the representative words before going on with the lesson.

2 Writing Words. On the lines below, write the words that you hear.

1. snake	5. respect	9. stable
2. smudge	6. stitch	10. sneeze
3. study	7. sleepy	11. smaller
4. slice	8. special	12. Spanish

3 Review of Doubling Patterns 1 and 2. Add the endings and write the words on the lines provided.

Part A. These words all end with one vowel and one final consonant. For the two-syllable words, you must determine if the last syllable is accented before deciding whether or not to double the final consonant.

1. hit + er	hitter	6. clip + ing	clipping
2. control + er	controller	7. drip + ing	dripping
3. forgot + en	forgotten	8. slip + er	slipper
4. trim + ed	trimmed	9. clot + ed	clotted
5. market + ing	marketing	10. admit + ance	admittance

Part B. Add the endings to these words. Double the final consonant when necessary.

1. repair + ed	repaired	6. forget + ing	forgetting
2. refer + al	referral	7. offer + ed	offered
3. invent + ing	inventing	8. fluster + ed	flustered
4. commit + ee	committee	9. prefer + ing	preferring
5. exert + ing	exerting	10. reject + ing	rejecting

Part C. Choose two of the words you formed and use them in sentences.

1. ______________________________

2. ______________________________

Lesson 4 17

2 Writing Words

Instruct students to write the words that you dictate, which are found on the replica of the student page. Say each word, use it in a phrase or simple sentence, and say the word again. Check to make sure students capitalize the *s* in *Spanish*.

3 Review of Doubling Patterns 1 and 2

When adding endings to the two-syllable words in Part A, students must determine which syllable is accented before deciding whether or not to double the final consonant. Emphasize that all of these words end with one vowel and one final consonant, so the only part of the pattern that they must consider is the accent.

If students want to verify their choice of the accented syllable, recommend that they check their dictionaries.

Part B includes a variety of words, and all three conditions of Doubling Pattern 2 must be analyzed before determining whether to double the final consonant.

Students may choose words from both Part A and Part B for the sentences they write in Part C. Challenge them to use two of the words in each sentence, for example they might write, "I keep *forgetting* to have my bike *repaired*."

Additional Exercise:

If students are having difficulty remembering the three conditions for Doubling Pattern 2, develop more exercises using a chart such as the one in Lesson 3. Then offer more practice without the chart.

4 Writing Words by Syllables. Write each word your teacher dictates by syllables. Then write the whole word on the line provided. Beside each syllable write the syllable type (C for closed, O for open, Cle for consonant plus *le*, VCe for vowel-consonant-*e*, or D for double vowel).

	First Syllable	Second Syllable	Third Syllable	Fourth Syllable	Whole Word
1.	stum C	ble Cle			stumble
2.	in C	spire VCe			inspire
3.	de O	spair D			despair
4.	snif C	fle Cle			sniffle
5.	spe O	cial D	ize VCe		specialize
6.	stim C	u O	late VCe		stimulate
7.	re O	spon C	si O	ble Cle	responsible
8.	spec C	tac C	u O	lar C	spectacular

5 The Possessive Form of Personal Pronouns. Pronouns have special forms that are used to show ownership or possession. These forms do not use an apostrophe, even though they may end in *s*. Study the examples below.

Singular Possessives		Plural Possessives
mine	his	ours
yours	hers	yours
	its	theirs

Write the sentences you hear.

1. Is his trip necessary?
2. The slipper is hers.
3. That glass is mine.
4. The snacks are theirs.
5. Is that sled yours?
6. That stuff is ours.
7. Where is the dog's bone?
8. Its bone is over there.

18 Lesson 4

4 Writing Words by Syllables

Remind students that the number of blanks for each word indicates the number of syllables in the word. Dictate each word on the replica of the student page syllable by syllable. Then pronounce the whole word normally.

Note any particular patterns with which students are having difficulty. Have them check any words they are not sure of in the dictionary.

Additional Activities:

Have students look up the meanings of any of these words that they don't already know.

Have them use some of the words in original sentences.

5 The Possessive Form of Personal Pronouns

This exercise is designed to call students' attention to the fact that no apostrophe is used to show possession with personal pronouns. With the exception of *its*, students are probably already using these words without any problems.

Go over the examples and point out the fact that none of these words has an apostrophe. Then dictate the short sentences on the replica of the student page.

6 Homonyms: *Its* and *It's*. Read the sentences below.

1. The kitten is chasing *its* tail.
2. You can't judge a book by *its* cover.
3. *It's* never too late.
4. It looks like *it's* going to rain.

Its is the possessive form of the pronoun *it*. Like other possessive pronouns, it does not need an apostrophe.

It's is the contraction for *it is*. Use the apostrophe only when you can substitute *it is* in the sentence.

Fill in either *its* or *it's* to complete the sentences below.

1. __It's__ snowing outside.
2. Please feed the dog __its__ dinner.
3. The snake has shed __its__ skin.
4. Do you know if __it's__ ten o'clock yet?
5. The spider caught a fly in __its__ web.
6. If __it's__ not one thing, __it's__ another.

7 Writing Sentences. On the lines below, write the sentences that you hear.

1. A snail carries its house on its back.
2. Do you know if those slippers are hers?
3. Steve spilled cereal all over the kitchen floor.
4. You can see the steel mill's smokestack from here.
5. Ted admitted he had forgotten to study for the exam.
6. Fran will be sneezing until her cold runs its course.
7. It's necessary to eat certain kinds of food every day.
8. Stan spent a year in Spain and speaks Spanish very well.

Lesson 4 19

6 Homonyms: *Its* and *It's*

This exercise gives students practice in choosing between *its* and *it's*. Emphasize that students must be able to say *it is* for *it's*. *It's* is a contraction. Suggest that whenever they write *its* or *it's*, they try to substitute *it is*.

Check to make sure students have capitalized *It's* in the first sentence.

7 Writing Sentences

Instruct students to write the sentences you dictate, which are on the replica of the student page. For the first few lessons, you may need to read some sentences twice. Encourage students to listen to the entire sentence and repeat it to themselves before they begin to write. This strategy will help them to develop their auditory memories.

These sentences give students an opportunity to write the sight words and some of the representative words in context. Note any specific errors that students make, and design additional words, sentences, or phrases for specific problems.

In addition to the blends covered in this lesson, the patterns found in these sentences include:
—possessive pronouns (1, 2, and 6)
—*its*/*it's* (1, 6, and 7)
—changing *y* to *i* (1)
—possessives (4)
—Doubling Pattern 2 (5)
—Silent *e* Pattern 1 (6)

Lesson 5

The Blends *sc*, *sk*, *sw*, and *tw*

Objectives

- **Blends:** Learn to spell words with the blends *sc*, *sk*, *sw*, and *tw*.
- **Sight Words:** Learn to spell *school*, *schedule*, *scene*, *scent*, *science*, and *scissors*. Discover that four of these words follow the soft *c* pattern.
- **Word Building:** Add initial blends to short- and long-vowel word families.
- **Alternative Spellings:** Learn that /sk/ at the beginning of words can be spelled three ways and that *sc* is the most common spelling.
- **Dictionary Skills:** Use the dictionary to find the correct spelling of words that start with /sk/.
- **Composing Sentences:** Write original sentences using selected words.
- **Words Related to *Two*:** Learn that *tw* at the beginning of words can signal the meaning *two*. Write the meanings of designated words that start with *tw* and *two*.
- **The Soft *c*:** Discover that *ce*, *ci*, and *cy* produce the soft *c*.
- **Homonyms:** Learn to discriminate between *principal* and *principle*.
- **Writing Sentences:** Practice writing representative and sight words in context.

Sight Words

Teach the sight words using the methods described on pages 9-12 in the introduction to this book. Point out that in two of these words, /sk/ is spelled *sch*. In the other four, *sc* spells /s/.

Lesson 5

The Blends *sc*, *sk*, *sw*, and *tw*

Sight Words		
school	scene	science
schedule	scent	scissors

Blends: *sc*, *sk*, *sw*, *tw*

1 Listening

Listen to the sound of *sc* in these words.

scab	scuff	score	scout
scar	scale	scare	scarlet
scum	scold	scarce	scatter

Listen to the sound of *sk* in these words.

skin	skirt	skull	sky
skip	skating	skillet	skiing

Listen to the sound of *sw* in these words.

swim	swell	Swiss	sweep
swam	swing	swear	sweet
swimming	switch	sweat	sweetheart

Listen to the sound of *tw* in these words.

twin	twelve	twist	tweed
twice	twenty	twitch	between
twine	twenty-five	twinkle	twilight

2 Writing Words. On the lines below, write the words that you hear.

1. skating	4. skill	7. swing
2. swimming	5. between	8. scarce
3. scuff	6. scared	9. twitch

20 Lesson 5

---

1 Listening

Point out that in the blend *sc*, both /s/ and /k/ are heard, in contrast to the digraph *sc* in the four sight words in which *sc* spells /s/. Then introduce the words with the blend *sc* using the following steps.

1. Say the sound /sk/ and ask students what letters make the sound in the first group of words.
2. Say the letters *s-c* and ask students what sound they make in those words.
3. Say the word *scab* and ask students what letters spell /sk/ and what letters spell /ab/.
4. Say the word *scab* and ask students what letters spell *scab*.

Follow the same steps to introduce the words with the blends *sk*, *sw*, and *tw*. Review any other patterns that students have already learned, such as the double *m* in *swimming* or the *ight* spelling of /īt/ in *twilight*.

Make sure that students know the meanings of all the representative words before going on with the lesson.

3 Word Building. Write one of the blends below in each blank to form a word. Do not make the same word twice.

sc *sk* *sw* *tw*

1. sw am	5. tw eed	9. sk in
2. sc are	6. tw ice	10. tw in
3. sk ate	7. sw im	11. sc old
4. sw ear	8. sk im	12. sc um

4 Dictionary Skills: Finding the Correct Spelling. In this lesson, the sound /sk/ is spelled three different ways. It is spelled *sk* as in *skip* and *skate*, *sc* as in *scab* and *scale*, and *sch* as in *scholar* and *schedule*. A dictionary can help you find the correct spelling of the /sk/ sound in a given word.

Use a dictionary to find the correct spelling of the words spelled phonetically below. The most common spelling for /sk/ is *sc*, so look for that first. When you find the word that has the meaning given, write the correct spelling on the line provided. The first one has been done to get you started.

Phonetic Spelling	Meaning	Correct Spelling
1. /skĕp´tĭk/	someone who doubts	skeptic
2. /skŭlp´tər/	an artist who works with stone or clay	sculptor
3. /skēm/	a plan or plot	scheme
4. /skăl´pəl/	a small knife used by doctors	scalpel
5. /skĕl´ə tən/	the bony framework of the body	skeleton
6. /skăv´ĭn jər/	an animal that feeds on dead things	scavenger

Use two of these words in sentences.

1. ______________________________

2. ______________________________

Lesson 5 21

2 Writing Words

Instruct students to write the words that you dictate, which are found on the replica of the student page. Say each word, use it in a phrase or simple sentence, and say the word again.

3 Word Building

In this exercise, students create words by adding blends to some of the word families from Books 1 and 2. Encourage them to use each blend at least once.

The answers given on the replica of the student page are examples. Accept all correctly spelled words.

4 Dictionary Skills: Finding the Correct Spelling

Before beginning this exercise, remind students that letters between slashes, e.g. /skab/, give the phonetic spelling of a word. Explain that a phonetic spelling represents the way a word is pronounced rather than the way it is spelled.

In this exercise, students determine the correct spelling of a sound that has alternative spellings by looking up the alternatives in the dictionary. Brief definitions of these words are given in the text, but students should understand that these will not match those in the dictionary exactly.

Go over the first item as a group so that students will understand what is required. If necessary, do the next one or two items together as well.

5 Words with *Two* in Their Meanings.

Many words that begin with the blend *tw* are related in some way to the number *two*. Explain how each of the words below is related to the number *two*.

1. twin — means one of two very similar or identical things
2. twice — means two times something; doing something two times
3. twelve — is two more than ten

Many compound words are built with *two*. Write the meanings of the words below on the lines provided. Use your dictionary if you need help.

1. two-edged — having an edge on both sides
2. two-faced — having two surfaces; also, deceitful or hypocritical
3. twosome — two people together; a couple
4. two-way — allowing passage in two directions

6 The Soft *c*.

When a *c* has the sound /s/, it is called a soft *c*. Look at the words below. Underline the soft *c* in each word. Then circle the letter that follows the soft *c*.

1. process	5. criticize	9. icy
2. necessary	6. citizen	10. juicy
3. excellent	7. society	11. bicycle
4. succeed	8. decision	12. cylinder

Fill in the blanks in the pattern below.

Pattern: When *c* is followed by e, i, or y, it has a soft /s/ sound.

7 Spelling Sight Words.

Four of the sight words in this lesson have the /s/ sound spelled *sc*. Write them on the lines below.

1. scene 2. scent 3. science 4. scissors

Circle the letter that comes after the *c* in these words.

Why is the *sc* pronounced /s/? The *c* is followed by *e* or *i*, so it is soft.

22 Lesson 5

5 Words with *Two* in Their Meanings

Before students begin this exercise, remind them that the *w* is not pronounced in the number *two*. Point out that it is pronounced in the related words *twin*, *twice*, and *twelve*.

You may want to have students work in pairs or small groups on this exercise.

Representative responses are given on the replica of the student page. Accept all responses that make sense.

Additional Activity:

Students might enjoy stretching their imaginations a bit by discussing the less obvious relationships to *two* in such words as *between*, *twine*, *twist*, *twilight*, and *twinkle*. Helping students to increase their interest in and awareness of words will help them to improve their spelling.

6 The Soft *c*

In this exercise, students discover that *c* is normally soft before *e*, *i*, and *y*. Point out that *c* makes a /k/ sound before other letters. The fact that *c* is soft before *e*, *i*, and *y* is a useful piece of information for both spelling and reading. This pattern also prepares students for Silent *e* Pattern 2, which is introduced in Lesson 11.

7 Spelling Sight Words

This exercise reinforces the soft *c* pattern discovered in Exercise 6. It also shows students that the *sc* spelling for /s/ in these sight words follows a regular pattern.

8 **Homonyms: *Principal* and *Principle*.** Look up the homonyms *principal* and *principle* in the dictionary and write a definition for each word on the lines below.

principal first in importance; the chief or main person or thing; the head of a school

principle a general rule or truth; a rule of personal conduct; a basic law of nature

Write either *principal(s)* or *principle(s)* in the blanks below.

1. There is a new principal at the high school.
2. I will vote for the candidate with the highest principles.
3. Grace was studying the principal parts of verbs.
4. He is one of the principal reporters for the newspaper.
5. Sir Isaac Newton studied the principle of gravity.
6. They discussed several basic principles at the meeting.

9 **Writing Sentences.** On the lines below, write the sentences that you hear.

1. May I use your scissors to cut this twine?
2. The children's mother scolded them for making a scene.
3. We smelled a very sweet scent coming from the kitchen.
4. Sid recycles everything he can as a matter of principle.
5. Twenty-five people will go skiing this weekend if it snows Thursday or Friday.
6. The school principal changed the schedule so the science class could take a special trip.

Lesson 5 23

8 Homonyms: *Principal* and *Principle*

Discuss the definitions that students write for these two homonyms before having them complete the sentences that follow.

If your students have difficulty completing the sentences, create additional sentences as needed until students understand these difficult homonyms.

Your students might be familiar with the mnemonic "The princi*pal* is a *pal*."

Some students may be helped if you point out that *principal* is a person and *principle* is an idea. Also, *principal* can be an adjective (as in "principal parts of verbs"), while *principle* is always a noun.

9 Writing Sentences

Instruct students to write the sentences you dictate, which are on the replica of the student page. For the first few lessons, you may need to read some sentences twice. Encourage students to listen to the entire sentence and repeat it to themselves before they begin to write. This strategy will help them to develop their auditory memories.

These sentences give students an opportunity to write the sight words and some of the representative words in context. Note any specific errors that students make, and design additional words, sentences, or phrases for specific problems.

In addition to the blends covered in this lesson, the patterns found in these sentences include:

—the soft *c* (1, 2, 3, 4, and 6)
—possessive pronouns (1)
—Silent *e* Pattern 1 (2, 3, and 6)
—alternative spellings of /sk/ (2, 5, and 6)
—possessives (2)
—homonyms (4 and 6)
—hyphenated numbers (5)

Review of Unit 1

Blends That Begin Syllables

Objectives

- **Word Building:** Add initial blends to short- and long-vowel word families.
- **Patterns:** Add endings to words and write dictated phrases following Doubling Patterns 1 and 2.
- **Possessives:** Write phrases containing possessive nouns. Use possessive pronouns to complete sentences.
- **Syllable Types:** Review five types of syllables by categorizing examples.
- **Writing by Syllables:** Write dictated words one syllable at a time.
- **Homonyms:** Review designated homonyms by using them in original sentences.
- **Alternative Spellings:** Review alternative spellings for /sk/.
- **Writing Sentences:** Practice writing representative and sight words in context.
- **Composing Paragraphs:** Write original paragraphs using representative words and sight words.
- **Puzzle:** Review representative words and sight words by completing a crossword puzzle.

Review of Unit 1

Blends That Begin Syllables

1 Word Building. Add one of the blends listed below to each of the word families to make a word. Do not make the same word twice.

bl	*pl*	*fr*	*sk*	*sp*
cl	*br*	*gr*	*sl*	*st*
fl	*cr*	*pr*	*sm*	*sw*
gl	*dr*	*tr*	*sn*	*tw*

1. cl ad	8. gr eet	15. cr ime
2. fl ag	9. sl eet	16. tw itch
3. br ag	10. tr ick	17. st ock
4. pr aise	11. sn iff	18. gl ow
5. sw am	12. sm ile	19. fr oze
6. pl ane	13. dr ill	20. st uff
7. bl eak	14. sp ill	21. sk unk

2 Review of Doubling Patterns 1 and 2

Part A. Add the endings and write the new words on the lines provided. Double the final consonant when necessary.

1. forbid + en	forbidden	7. tax + able	taxable
2. swim + er	swimmer	8. twist + ing	twisting
3. admit + ance	admittance	9. drug + ist	druggist
4. stop + ing	stopping	10. scarce + ly	scarcely
5. commit + ee	committee	11. spot + ed	spotted
6. commit + ment	commitment	12. begin + er	beginner

24 Review of Unit 1

1 Word Building

In this exercise, students create words by adding blends from Unit 1 to word families studied in Books 1 and 2. Encourage them to use as many of the blends as they can.

The answers given on the replica of the student page are examples. There are a number of other correct responses. Accept any correctly spelled word.

2 Review of Doubling Patterns 1 and 2

Review Doubling Patterns 1 and 2 before students begin this exercise. Emphasize that in words of two or more syllables, the final consonant is doubled *only* when the last syllable has a short vowel and a single consonant, is accented, and the ending starts with a vowel.

Be sure to dictate the phrases in Part B slowly enough that students who need to analyze the word will have time to do so.

Part B. On the lines below, write the phrases that you hear.

1. forgetting your manners
2. beginning to understand
3. admitted we were right
4. offering to help
5. expelled from the country
6. a committee meeting

❸ **The Possessive Apostrophe.** Rewrite the phrases below using an apostrophe to show ownership or possession.

1. the club of the boys — the boys' club
2. the car of the Browns — the Browns' car
3. the responsibility of the country — the country's responsibility
4. the bicycle of Dennis — Dennis's bicycle
5. the softness of the blanket — the blanket's softness
6. the son of Triana — Triana's son
7. the last glow of twilight — twilight's last glow
8. the problem of the Brelands — the Brelands' problem
9. the rights of women — women's rights
10. the honor of the scout — the scout's honor

❹ **Possessive Pronouns.** Fill in the blanks in the sentences below with the appropriate word.

1. The ice cream belongs to us. It is ours.
2. The truck belongs to them. It is theirs.
3. Those gloves belong to her. They are hers.
4. That ring has lost its glitter.
5. That present belongs to you. It is yours.
6. The swing belongs to him. It is his.

Review of Unit 1 25

❸ The Possessive Apostrophe

These phrases review the use of the possessive apostrophe. Before beginning the exercise, review the three steps used to decide where to place the possessive apostrophe and whether or not to add an *s*.

❹ Possessive Pronouns

If necessary, review the possessive pronouns listed in Lesson 4, Exercise 5 before students begin this exercise. Be sure they understand that they are to fill in a possessive pronoun to complete each sentence.

5 **Review of Syllable Types.** Write each syllable below on a line under the correct heading.

deem	fle	be	pock	gle
hap	tac	ci	o	tone
train	mote	cle	sime	ceal

Closed	Open	Cle
1. hap	1. be	1. fle
2. tac	2. ci	2. cle
3. pock	3. o	3. gle

VCe	Double Vowel
1. mote	1. deem
2. sime	2. train
3. tone	3. ceal

6 **Writing Words by Syllables.** Write each word your teacher dictates by syllables. Then write the whole word on the line provided.

	First Syllable	Second Syllable	Third Syllable	Fourth Syllable	Whole Word
1.	ruf	fle			ruffle
2.	tri	an	gle		triangle
3.	e	lec	tric		electric
4.	drag	on	fly		dragonfly
5.	pro	gres	sive		progessive
6.	dra	mat	ic		dramatic
7.	sta	bil	i	ty	stability
8.	es·	pe	cial	ly	especially

26 Review of Unit 1

5 Review of Syllable Types

If necessary, review the attributes of each syllable type before students begin this exercise.

6 Writing Words by Syllables

Remind students that the number of blanks for each word indicates the number of syllables in the word. Dictate each word on the replica of the student page syllable by syllable. Then pronounce the whole word normally.

Note any particular patterns with which students are having difficulty. Have them check any words they are not sure of in the dictionary.

Additional Activities:

Have students identify the types of syllables they have written by using C for closed, O for open, VCe for vowel-consonant-*e*, Cle for consonant plus *le*, or D for double vowel syllables.

Have students look up the meanings of any of these words that they don't already know.

Have them use some of the words in original sentences.

7 Review of Homonyms. Write a sentence using each of the homonyms below.

1. its ______
2. it's ______
3. principal ______
4. principle ______

8 Alternative Spellings for /sk/. Below are three ways to spell /sk/. On the lines under each heading, write words that use those letters to spell /sk/.

sc	sk	sch
1. scab	1. skate	1. school
2. scare	2. skin	2. schedule
3. scold	3. skip	3. scheme
4. scout	4. sky	
5. scuff		
6. scatter		

9 Writing Sentences. Write the sentences that you hear.

1. Grace's trip to France last April was truly special.
2. She traveled by plane from San Francisco.
3. She drove around the country with two friends from home.
4. They stayed in small towns and explored the countryside.
5. The car got stuck twice, and then its clutch broke.
6. Grace was afraid she'd miss her flight back to America.
7. A truck driver agreed to rush them to the plane.
8. Now Grace is planning to fly to Spain in February.

Review of Unit 1 27

7 Review of Homonyms

If necessary, review the meanings of these homonyms before students compose sentences using each of them.

8 Alternative Spellings for /sk/

Three ways to spell /sk/ are reviewed in this exercise. Notice that six *sc* words are asked for, while only four *sk* words and three *sch* words are required. This is to remind students that *sc* is the most common spelling for /sk/ and *sch* is the least common.

The answers on the replica of the student page are examples. Accept all correctly spelled words under each heading. Check to be sure there are no soft *c* words, such as *science*, in the *sc* column.

9 Writing Sentences

Instruct students to write the sentences that you dictate, which are on the replica of the student page. Note any specific errors. Design additional sentences, words, or phrases for specific problems.

Patterns found in these sentences include:

—soft *c* (1, 2, and 5)
—possessive (1)
—Silent *e* Pattern 1 (4)
—compound words (4)
—possessive pronouns (5)
—contractions (6)
—Doubling Pattern 1 (8)

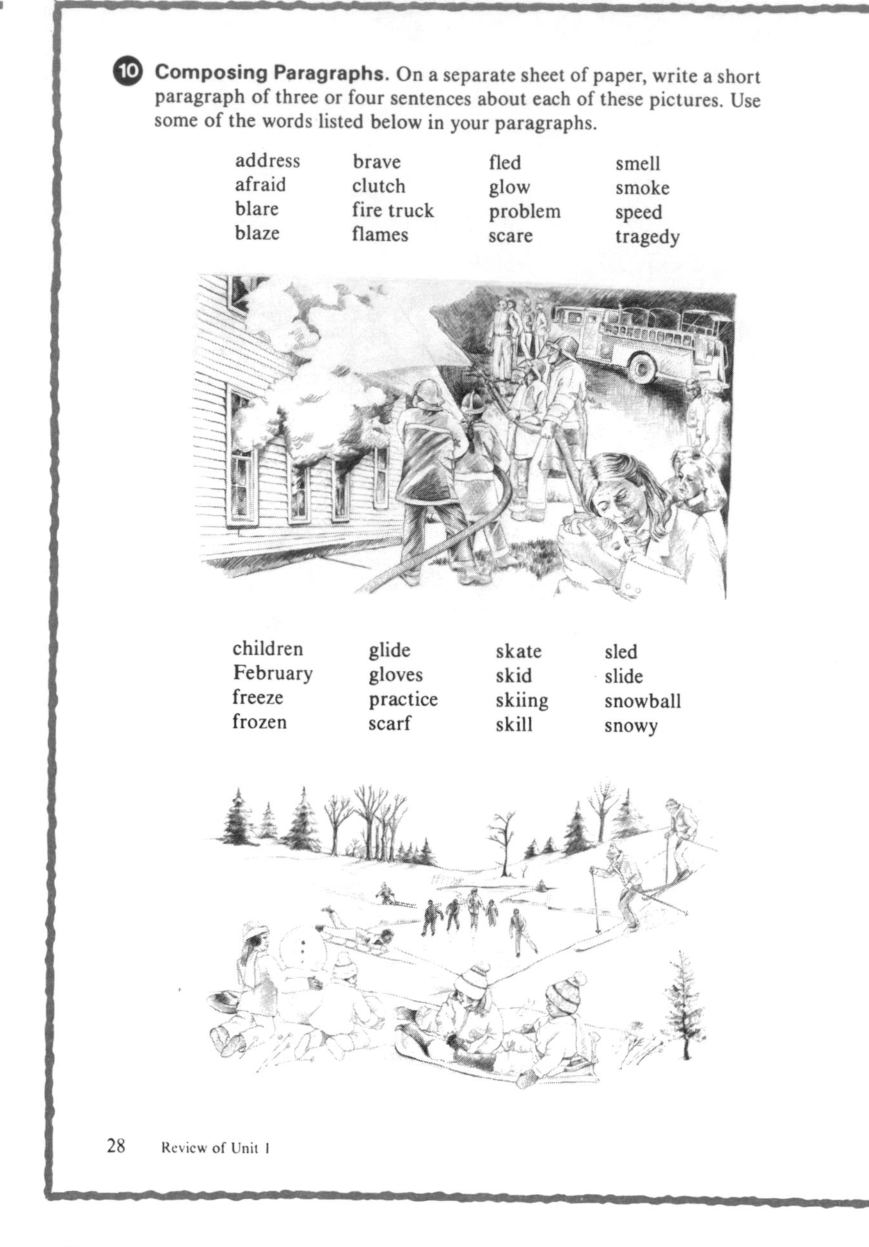

10 Composing Paragraphs. On a separate sheet of paper, write a short paragraph of three or four sentences about each of these pictures. Use some of the words listed below in your paragraphs.

address	brave	fled	smell
afraid	clutch	glow	smoke
blare	fire truck	problem	speed
blaze	flames	scare	tragedy

children	glide	skate	sled
February	gloves	skid	slide
freeze	practice	skiing	snowball
frozen	scarf	skill	snowy

28 Review of Unit 1

10 Composing Paragraphs

Encourage students to write as much as they can about these pictures. It is important for students to recognize that their spelling has improved and that this, in turn, has resulted in more fluent writing.

Discuss the illustrations with students before they begin to write their paragraphs. This will help them to develop ideas to write about before trying to write.

Do not discourage students from using words that are troublesome. They should have access to a dictionary for all free writing activities. Encourage students to look up words they are not sure of after they finish writing. Discuss how to find those words in a dictionary.

Remember that errors in words that have not yet been studied shouldn't be treated negatively. Point out any parts of the word that are spelled correctly and praise the effort. This exercise is intended to provide positive reinforcement for students, so it is important to emphasize the correctly spelled portions of misspelled words.

⓫ Crossword Puzzle. Use the clues below to complete this crossword puzzle. Most of the answers are representative words or sight words from Unit 1 or contain the Unit 1 blends.

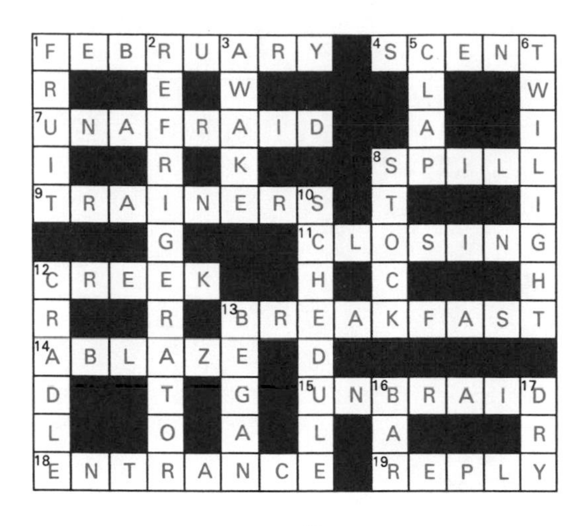

Across

1. The second month
4. An odor or smell
7. Not scared
8. Cause to run out: Don't ___ the beans.
9. People who teach boxers
11. The opposite of opening
12. A small stream
13. The first meal of the day
14. Afire, blazing
15. To take out a braid
18. A doorway
19. To answer

Down

1. Peaches and apples are two types of ___.
2. An appliance that keeps food cold
3. Not asleep
5. Applaud
6. The time between sunset and full night
8. A supply kept on hand
10. A timetable; a list of times
12. What a baby is rocked in
13. Started
16. To block from entering
17. Not wet

Review of Unit 1 29

⓫ Crossword Puzzle

Have students complete the crossword puzzle. Tell them that most of the answer words are representative or sight words from Unit 1. The clues are mostly definitions that rely on the students' general knowledge.

Allow students to use a dictionary if they want to. You might want them to work in pairs or small groups. If necessary, give them the following list of answer words and have them check off words as they use them.

For 14 across, both *ablaze* and *aflame* fit the spaces and the clue. Accept either as a correct answer.

ablaze *or* aflame
awake
bar
began
breakfast
clap
closing
cradle
creek
dry
entrance
February
fruit
refrigerator
reply
scent
schedule
spill
stock
trainers
twilight
unafraid
unbraid

Unit 1 Tests

We recommend that you test your students on the representative words and sight words from Unit 1 before going on. The following are suggested lists of representative words and sight words from Unit 1. You may want to substitute other words to meet the needs of your students.

Dictate each word and use it in a simple sentence. Students should be able to spell 90 percent of these words correctly.

Representative Words	Sight Words
1. black	1. food
2. brain	2. America
3. agree	3. million
4. frog	4. juice
5. crack	5. fruit
6. price	6. refrigerator
7. dream	7. salad
8. train	8. spaghetti
9. stable	9. chocolate
10. respect	10. necessary
11. snack	11. cereal
12. smile	12. iron
13. slap	13. house
14. skating	14. schedule
15. scuff	15. scissors
16. sweet	16. scene
17. twin	17. school
18. brush	18. science
19. clock	19. build
20. green	20. certain

Lesson 6

The Digraph *sh* and the Suffixes *-tion*, *-sion*, and *-cian*

Objectives

- **Digraph and Suffixes:** Learn to spell words with the diagraph *sh* and the suffixes *-tion*, *-sion*, and *-cian.*
- **Sight Words:** Learn to spell *sure*, *sugar*, *ocean*, *suspicion*, *cushion*, and *fashion*.
- **Word Building:** Write the missing syllables of dictated words.
- **Alternative Spellings:** Learn that /shən/ at the end of words can be spelled three ways and that *-tion* is the most common spelling.
- **Suffixes:** Add *-tion* to verbs to create nouns.
  Add *-cian* to root words.
- **Composing Sentences:** Write original sentences using selected words.
- **Root Words:** Identify root verbs from which words ending in *-sion* were built.
- **Patterns:** Discover that *-cian* is often added to words that end in *ic* or *ics.*
  Discover certain generalizations about predicting the spelling of /sh/.
- **Writing by Syllables:** Write dictated words one syllable at a time.
- **Writing Sentences:** Practice writing representative and sight words in context.

Sight Words

Teach the sight words using the methods described on pages 9-12 in the introduction to this book.

Lesson 6

The Digraph *sh* and the Suffixes *-tion*, *-sion*, and *-cian*

Sight Words		
sure	ocean	cushion
sugar	suspicion	fashion

Digraph: *sh*
Suffixes: *-tion*, *-sion*, *-cian*

1 Listening

Listen to the sound of *sh* in these words.

she	shoe	shady	wish
shall	should	shears	flesh
shacks	shoulder	shining	blush

Listen to the sound of *-tion* in these words.

action	addition	attention	donation
fiction	inflation	imagination	vacation
station	pollution	occupation	transportation

Listen to the sound of *-sion* in these words.

session	admission	expression	division
profession	permission	discussion	television

Listen to the sound of *-cian* in these words.

magician	beautician	musician	optician

2 Writing Words. On the lines below, write the words that you hear.

1. action	4. attention	7. television
2. wish	5. shoulder	8. shell
3. session	6. station	9. beautician

30 Lesson 6

Each of these words contains the sound /sh/ spelled in an unusual way. *Ocean* and *sugar* were sight words in Book 2 and are reviewed here because of the /sh/ sound.

Point out that in *sure* and *sugar*, /sh/ is spelled *su. Ocean* and a very few scientific words use *ce* to spell /sh/. *Suspicion* contains the unusual ending *cion.* Finally, *fashion* and *cushion* are the only English words that end in *shion.*

1 Listening

Explain to students that a digraph is a combination of two letters that represents one sound. Sometimes a digraph is an alternative spelling for a sound that can be spelled with a single letter, as when *ck* spells /k/ or *dg* spells /j/. Sometimes, however, a digraph represents a new sound, such as /sh/ and /ch/.

Introduce the words with the digraph *sh* using the following steps.

1. Say the sound /sh/ and ask students what letters make the sound.
2. Say the letters *s-h* and ask students what sound they make.
3. Say the word *she* and ask students what letters spell /sh/ and what letter spells /ē/.

3 Words That End in *-tion*. The letters *tion* at the end of a word are pronounced /shən/. The most common way to spell /shən/ is *tion*. With the exception of *fashion* and *cushion*, /shən/ is not spelled *shion*. Listen to the following words and write the missing syllables.

1. va ca tion	6. po si tion
2. con di tion	7. in ven tion
3. so lu tion	8. nu tri tion
4. sub trac tion	9. con cen tra tion
5. trans la tion	10. e val u a tion

4 Word Building with *-tion*. The suffix *-tion* is a very common suffix. It is often used to change verbs into nouns. Sometimes when *-tion* is added, the root word changes or some other letters are added, but you can usually hear the changes.

Example: concentrate + tion = concentration

Add *-tion* to these verbs. Pronounce the new word before you spell it. Use the dictionary to check your spellings. The first one has been done to get you started.

1. situate + tion	situation	6. operate + tion	operation
2. designate + tion	designation	7. frustrate + tion	frustration
3. create + tion	creation	8. expire + tion	expiration
4. educate + tion	education	9. explain + tion	explanation
5. illustrate + tion	illustration	10. devote + tion	devotion

Use three of the new words in sentences.

1. ____________________
2. ____________________
3. ____________________

Lesson 6 31

4. Say the word *she* and ask students what letters spell *she*.

Follow the same steps to introduce the words with the suffixes *-tion*, *-sion*, and *-cian*. Point out that *-tion*, *-sion*, and *-cian* all spell /shən/.

When introducing words of three or more syllables, have students spell each part of the word before asking them to spell the whole word. Introduce these words as follows.

1. Say the sound /shən/ and ask students what letters make the sound in the first group of words.
2. Say the letters *t-i-o-n* and ask students what sound they make.
3. Say the word *inflation* and ask students what letters spell /in/, what letters spell /fl/, what letter spells /ā/, and what letters spell /shən/.
4. Say the word *inflation* and ask students what letters spell *inflation*.

When introducing the words ending in *-sion*, draw attention to the words that have a double *s*. Point out to students that both *s*'s are needed to spell the word, even though there is no /s/ sound in the word.

Make sure that students know the meanings of all the representative words before going on with the lesson.

2 Writing Words

Instruct students to write the words that you dictate, which are found on the replica of the student page. Say each word, use it in a phrase or simple sentence, and say the word again.

3 Words That End in -*tion*

This exercise requires students to isolate and spell single syllables. Dictate the entire word, giving students time to isolate the missing syllable and write it in the blank. Emphasize that *-tion* is the most common way to spell /shən/. Have students look up the meanings of any of these words they don't know.

Additional Activity:

Have students use some of these words in sentences of their own.

4 Word Building With -*tion*

In this exercise, students add *-tion* to verbs, changing them into nouns. Go over the example and number 1 to be sure students see that *te* has been dropped in *concentration* and *situation*. Stress the fact that they can hear these changes when the words are pronounced.

Have students add *-tion* to each of the verbs. When students have completed this part of the exercise, go over their answers with them and be sure they can tell what letters change or are dropped in each root word.

Be sure students know the meanings of all of the words they formed before they try to use them in original sentences.

5 Words That End in *-sion*. The most common way to spell /shən/ at the end of a word is *-tion*. The next most likely way to spell the ending /shən/ is *-sion*. The suffix *-sion* can also be used to change verbs into nouns. Listen to the following words and write the missing syllables.

1. con fes sion
2. re vi sion
3. pro vi sion
4. im pres sion
5. re ces sion
6. pro ces sion
7. sup er vi sion
8. col li sion
9. com mis sion

Use three of the words above in sentences.

1. ______
2. ______
3. ______

6 Root Words. Write the root word from which each of the words in Exercise 5 was built.

1. confess
2. revise
3. provide
4. impress
5. recess
6. process
7. supervise
8. collide
9. commit

7 Word Building with the Suffix *-cian*. The suffix *-cian* is usually added to words to indicate a person who does some skilled work. Add the suffix *-cian* to the root words below to make a word meaning a person who has skill in a particular area. Use the dictionary to check your spellings.

1. magic + cian magician
2. statistics + cian statistician
3. pediatrics + cian pediatrician
4. politics + cian politician
5. electric + cian electrician
6. mathematics + cian mathematician

Look at the root words above and fill in the blanks in the following pattern.

Pattern: Words that end in *-cian* often have roots that end in ic or ics.

32 Lesson 6

5 Words That End in *-sion*

This exercise is similar to Exercise 3 and should be done the same way. Again, be sure students know the meaning of each of these words before writing their sentences.

6 Root Words

In this exercise, students can see the relationship between the noun and verb forms of these words. Point out the roots that end in *ss*, and note that *-sion* is often used with root words that end in *ss*.

There is no foolproof pattern for predicting whether a /shən/ suffix will be spelled *-tion* or *-sion*, but remind students that *-tion* is the more common ending.

7 Word Building with the Suffix *-cian*

This exercise introduces the third common spelling for /shən/, *-cian*. Explain that this suffix usually denotes a person who has a skill in a particular area.

The pattern reveals that most words that end in *-cian* come from roots ending in *ic* or *ics*. If students are confused about how many letters to include in this pattern, explain that they should include all the letters that are common to all the root words, i.e., *ic* and *ics* but not *tics* or *tric*.

You may want to point out that the representative word *beautician* has a root word that ends in *y* and doesn't follow this pattern.

Additional Activity:

Have students look up the meanings of any of these words that they don't know.

8 Discovering a Pattern. In the representative words in this lesson, the sound /sh/ is spelled four different ways: *sh, ti, si,* and *ci.* Think about the representative words you have studied and fill in the blanks in the pattern below.

Pattern: At the beginning or end of a word, /sh/ is usually spelled sh. Syllables pronounced /shən/ can be spelled tion, sion, or cian. The most common spelling of /shən/ is tion.

9 Writing Words by Syllables. Write each word your teacher dictates by syllables. Then write the whole word on the line provided.

	First Syllable	Second Syllable	Third Syllable	Fourth Syllable	Whole Word
1.	na	tion			nation
2.	am	bi	tion		ambition
3.	im	pres	sion		impression
4.	cre	a	tion		creation
5.	re	vi	sion		revision
6.	pol	i	ti	cian	politician
7.	con	ver	sa	tion	conversation
8.	il	lus	tra	tion	illustration
9.	ex	pla	na	tion	explanation

10 Writing Sentences. On the lines below, write the sentences that you hear.

1. Today's discussion is about the pollution of our oceans.
2. I have a suspicion she should pay more attention in school.
3. The beautician cut Shirley's hair in the latest fashion.
4. We sat on cushions and watched television at Stan's house.
5. Are you sure you added sugar and spices to the fruit cake?

Lesson 6 33

8 Discovering a Pattern

This pattern summarizes some of the information about the various spellings of /sh/.

When students have filled in the blanks in the pattern, remind them that *-sion* is often added to words that end in double *s* and that *-cian* indicates a person skilled in some work. All of this information provides useful strategies for predicting the spelling of /shən/ in words they haven't studied.

9 Writing Words by Syllables

Remind students that the number of blanks for each word indicates the number of syllables in the word. Dictate each word on the replica of the student page syllable by syllable. Then pronounce the whole word normally.

Note any particular patterns with which students are having difficulty. Have them check any words they are not sure of in the dictionary.

Students who have difficulty spelling three- and four-syllable words may find it helpful to identify the syllable types. Encourage them to pronounce the words syllable by syllable. For students who continue to have difficulty, pronounce the words by syllables and ask them to spell each syllable after you say it.

Additional Activities:

Have students look up the meanings of any of these words that they don't already know.

Have them use some of the words in original sentences.

10 Writing Sentences

Instruct students to write the sentences you dictate, which are on the replica of the student page.

These sentences give students an opportunity to write the sight words and some of the representative words in context. Note any specific errors that students make, and design additional words, sentences, or phrases for specific problems.

In addition to the blends covered in this lesson, the patterns found in these sentences include:

—words that end in /shən/ (1, 2, 3, and 4)
—possessives (1, 3, and 4)
—possessive pronouns (1)

Lesson 7

The Digraphs *ph* and *ch* and the Suffix *-ture*

Objectives

- **Digraphs and Suffix:** Learn to spell words with the diagraphs *ph* and *ch* and the suffix *-ture*.
- **Sight Words:** Learn to spell the words *psychology*, *psychologist*, *natural*, *spatula*, *chef*, and *machine*.
- **Etymology:** Learn that *ch* spells /k/ in words of Greek origin and that *ch* spells /sh/ in words of French origin.
- **Word Roots:** Learn the meaning of the root *psych-*.
- **Composing Sentences:** Write original sentences using selected and designated words.
- **Alternative Spellings:** Learn that /chur/ can be spelled *ture* or *cher* and that *ture* is the more common spelling.
- **Word Building:** Fill in *ture* or *cher* to spell words in context.
- **Possessives:** Write phrases containing possessive nouns.
- **Writing Sentences:** Practice writing representative and sight words in context.
- **Puzzle:** Use words with digraphs and suffixes to complete a puzzle.

Lesson 7

The Digraphs *ph* and *ch* and the Suffix *-ture*

Sight Words		
psychology	natural	chef
psychologist	spatula	machine

1 Listening

Digraphs

ph — Listen to the sound of *ph* in these words.

phone	physical	alphabet
phony	physician	telephone
phobia	photograph	microphone

ch as /ch/ — Listen to the sound of *ch* in these words.

check	chain	reach	rich
child	cheap	bleach	speech
chance	cheese	teacher	merchant

ch as /k/ — Listen to the sound of *ch* in these words.

chemical	chorus	ache
character	technical	anchor
Christmas	technician	stomach

Suffix *-ture* — Listen to the sound of *-ture* in these words.

feature	nature	adventure	lecture
fracture	picture	agriculture	mixture

2 Writing Words. On the lines below, write the words that you hear.

1. alphabet	4. ache	7. physical
2. cheap	5. teacher	8. character
3. peach	6. feature	9. adventure

34 Lesson 7

Sight Words

Teach the sight words using the methods described on pages 9-12 in the introduction to this book. Point out that in *psychology* and *psychologist*, /k/ is spelled *ch* and that the initial *p* is silent. Also note the *ch* spelling of /sh/ in *chef* and *machine* and the *tu* spelling of /ch/ in *natural* and *spatula*.

1 Listening

Introduce the words with the digraph *ph* using the following steps.

1. Say the sound /f/ and ask students what letters make the sound in the first group of words.
2. Say the letters *p-h* and ask students what sound they make.
3. Say the word *phone* and ask students what letters spell /f/ and what letters spell /ōn/.
4. Say the word *phone* and ask students what letters spell *phone*.

Follow the same steps to introduce the words with the digraph *ch* and the suffix *-ture*.

When introducing words that have many phonemes, such as *photograph*, have students spell each part of the word before spelling the whole word. Use the following steps.

1. Say the sound /f/ and ask students what letters make the sound.
2. Say the letters *p-h* and ask students what sound they make.
3. Say the word *photograph* and ask students what letters spell /f/, what letter spells /ō/, what letters spell /tō/, what letters spell /gr/, what letter spells /ă/, and what letters spell /f/.
4. Say the word *photo* and ask students what letters spell *photo*.
5. Say the word *graph* and ask students what letters spell *graph*.
6. Say the word *photograph* and ask students what letters spell *photograph*.

3 **Dictionary Skills: Word Origins.** Words have come into English from many different languages. Sometimes knowing what language a word comes from will help you remember how to spell it. Many dictionaries list the origins of root words. Look up the words below and write the language from which each came on the line beside it.

1. character Greek
2. stomach Greek
3. technology Greek
4. chef French
5. brochure French
6. chauvinism French

Now fill in the blanks in this pattern.

Ch often spells /k/ in words taken from Greek.

Ch often spells /sh/ in words taken from French.

4 **The Roots *psych-* and *psycho-***

1. Write the words that you hear.

psychology psychologist

What language do these words probably come from? Greek

How do you know? ch spells /k/

2. Look up the root *psych-* or *psycho-* and write the meaning on the line below.

The root psych- or psycho- refers to the mind.

3. Write two other words that have *psych-* or *psycho-* as a root.

psychiatry psychosis

4. Use one of these words in a sentence.

____

____

Lesson 7 35

Review any patterns in individual words that students have already studied. Point out that *ph* and *ch* can occur at both the beginning and end of syllables.

Make sure that students know the meanings of all the representative words before going on with the lesson.

2 Writing Words

Instruct students to write the words that you dictate, which are found on the replica of the student page. Say each word, use it in a phrase or simple sentence, and say the word again.

3 Dictionary Skills: Word Origins

The purpose of this exercise is to make students aware that sometimes features that appear to be irregularities in our language are really predictable variations based on etymology.

Not all dictionaries give information on word origins, and those that do may not agree. You may want students to do this exercise as a group and have them share the information that they find and discuss any variations.

Help your students find the information on word origins in their dictionaries. Some dictionaries list the origin of a word directly after the phonetic spelling of the word, while others list it after the definitions of the word. Word origins are usually enclosed in brackets: [ ].

You will also need to help students interpret the information they find, particularly the abbreviations used and the symbol <, which means *from.*

Some dictionaries will list only the language in which the word originated, i.e., *Gr.* for *Greek* or *Fr.* for *French.* Others will indicate the path a word took to get from the original language into English. For instance, students might find the listing [ME < OFr. < Lat. < Gk], which means that the word went from Greek into Latin, then into Old French, then into Middle English, and finally into present-day English. If students' dictionaries contain this level of information, explain that the last language listed is the language in which the word originated.

Point out also that information on the origin of the word will be given only for the root or root word and not for words built from the root. For instance, the Greek origin will be listed for *character* but not for *characteristic* or *characterize.*

4 The Roots *psych-* and *psycho-*

This exercise introduces the root *psych-* and reviews the relationship between the Greek origin of the root and the spelling of /k/ in the root.

5 Word Building: Alternative Spellings for /chur/. The most common way to spell /chur/ at the end of a word is *ture*. However, when *-er* is added to a word that ends in *ch*, then /chur/ is spelled *cher*. Fill in the blanks in the sentences below with *ture* or *cher*. Use your dictionary, if necessary.

1. The sick child had a very high tempera_t_ _u_ _r_ _e_.
2. Do you ever wish you could know what the fu_t_ _u_ _r_ _e_ will bring?
3. Our softball team needs a new pit_c_ _h_ _e_ _r_ and a new cat_c_ _h_ _e_ _r_.
4. The company Chuck works for has begun to manufac_t_ _u_ _r_ _e_ blea_c_ _h_ _e_ _r_s.
5. The legisla_t_ _u_ _r_ _e_ passed the bill and sent it to the governor for his signa_t_ _u_ _r_ _e_.

6 The Possessive Apostrophe. Rewrite the phrases below using an apostrophe to show ownership or possession.

1. the beauty of nature — nature's beauty
2. the features of the twins — the twins' features
3. the office of the physician — the physician's office
4. the room of the teachers — the teachers' room
5. the temperature of the child — the child's temperature
6. the adventure of the scouts — the scouts' adventure

7 Writing Sentences. On the lines below, write the sentences that you hear.

1. This photograph of Phil is so natural.
2. The chef flipped the pancakes with a spatula.
3. Fran's speech teacher knows a lot about psychology.
4. The psychologist talked with Chuck about his phobia.
5. The technician explained the features of the machine.

36 Lesson 7

5 Word Building: Alternative Spellings for /chur/

In this exercise, students must choose between two spellings for /chur/. Emphasize that *ture* is more common than *cher*.

The *cher* spelling usually is a result of an *-er* ending added to a word that ends in *ch*. Tell students to test for the *cher* spelling by dropping the /ur/. If they can remove the /ur/ and still have a word, /chur/ is probably spelled *cher*. Model this for them with *teacher* and *nature*. *Teacher* minus /ur/ is /tĕch/, but *nature* minus /ur/ is /nāch/, which isn't a word.

6 The Possessive Apostrophe

These phrases review the use of the possessive apostrophe. Before beginning the exercise, review the three steps used to decide where to place the apostrophe and whether or not to add an *s*.

7 Writing Sentences

Instruct students to write the sentences that you dictate, which are on the replica of the student page.

These sentences give students an opportunity to write the sight words and some of the representative words in context. Note any specific errors that students make, and design additional words, sentences, or phrases for specific problems.

In addition to the blends covered in this lesson, the patterns found in these sentences include:
—Doubling Pattern 1 (2)
—possessives (3)
—words ending in /chur/ (3 and 5)
—words ending in /shən/ (5)

8 Puzzle. Match the clues below with words from the list at the right. Use the words to fill in the blocks of the puzzle. When you have filled in all the correct answers, the shaded blocks will spell a new word ending in *-ture*. The first one has been done to get you started.

Clues

1. a group of lawmakers
2. something created or made up
3. to use machinery to make something
4. an exciting or difficult experience
5. a speech given to teach or inform
6. a desire to succeed or achieve something
7. a photograph or drawing of something
8. the exchange of ideas and opinions
9. a doctor who treats children
10. to break or crack

Word List

adventure
ambition
discussion
fracture
invention
lecture
✓legislature
manufacture
pediatrician
picture

1. L E G I S L A T U R E
2. I N V E N T I O N
3. M A N U F A C T U R E
4. A D V E N T U R E
5. L E C T U R E
6. A M B I T I O N
7. P I C T U R E
8. D I S C U S S I O N
9. P E D I A T R I C I A N
10. F R A C T U R E

Write the new word ending in *-ture*: LITERATURE

Use this new word in a sentence. Use your dictionary if you need to.

____

____

Lesson 7 37

8 Puzzle

In this type of puzzle, each row of blocks represents one answer word. Students are to write one letter of the answer word in each block. Clues are numbered to correspond to the rows of blocks. An alphabetized list of answer words is provided.

Go over the first clue and the filled-in answer so students will understand how to do the puzzle.

When all of the answers have been filled in, the shaded blocks will spell the word *literature* vertically. Have students write this word on the line provided and use it in a sentence.

Lesson 8

The Digraphs *th* and *wh*

Objectives

- **Digraphs:** Learn to spell words with the digraphs *th* and *wh*.
- **Sight Words:** Learn to spell *thought*, *Thomas*, *whose*, *whoever*, *wear*, and *weather*. Learn to distinguish *wear* and *weather* from words that sound almost the same.
- **Suffixes:** Learn to form ordinal numbers by adding *-th* or *-eth.*
- **Plural Apostrophe:** Use the apostrophe to form plurals of letters and abbreviations.
- **Contractions:** Review forming contractions.
- **Homonyms:** Learn to discriminate among *their, there,* and *they're.*
- **Composing a Letter:** Write an original letter using representative words and sight words.
- **Writing Sentences:** Practice writing representative and sight words in context.

Lesson 8

The Digraphs *th* and *wh*

Sight Words		
thought	whose	wear
Thomas	whoever	weather

Digraphs

❶ Listening

th as /th/

Listen to the sound of *th* in these words.

thick	thank	both	tooth
thirsty	think	bath	truth
thunder	thirteen	athletic	anything

th as /*th*/

Listen to the sound of *th* in these words.

than	there	thus	smooth
that	their	these	brother
this	themselves	though	together

wh

Listen to the sound of *wh* in these words.

why	where	whip	whether
when	which	wheel	whistle
what	whichever	white	awhile

❷ Writing Words. On the lines below, write the words that you hear.

1. think
2. these
3. awhile
4. thirsty
5. whistle
6. together
7. smooth
8. tooth
9. whisper

38 Lesson 8

Sight Words

Teach the sight words using the methods described on pages 9-12 in the introduction to this book. Draw attention to the *ough* in *thought* and the *th* spelling of /t/ in *Thomas*. Point out that *whose* and *whoever* contain the Book 1 sight words *who*. Draw attention to the different pronunciations of *ea* in *wear* and *weather*.

❶ Listening

Point out to students the two sounds of *th*. In the first group of words, the /th/ is unvoiced. The second group of words contains the voiced /*th*/.

Introduce the words with the unvoiced *th* using the following steps.

1. Say the sound /th/ and ask students what letters make the sound.
2. Say the letters *t-h* and ask students what sound they make.
3. Say the word *thick* and ask students what letters spell /th/ and what letters spell /ik/.
4. Say the word *thick* and ask students what letters spell *thick*.

Follow the same steps to introduce the words with the voiced *th* and the digraph *wh*.

Mention to students that *wh* is usually pronounced *h-w*, although in some regions, *wh* is pronounced /w/.

Make sure that students know the meanings of all the representative words before going on with the lesson.

❷ Writing Words

Instruct students to write the words that you dictate, which are found on the replica of the student page. Say each word, use it in a phrase or simple sentence, and say the word again.

3 Words That Sound Almost Alike. Underline the word that you hear in each pair.

1. weather — whether 2. wear — where

These pairs of words sound almost alike, but their meanings are very different. Fill in the correct word to complete each sentence below.

1. Thomas doesn't like to ___wear___ a necktie.
2. Let me know ___whether___ or not you can come to dinner.
3. Do you remember ___where___ you put the picture frames?
4. I hope the ___weather___ is fine for your picnic tomorrow.

4 Numbers That End in *th*. Numbers that end in *th* are used to indicate the position of something in a series. Sometimes the spelling of the root number changes when *th* is added. When the root number ends in *ty*, the *y* is changed to *i* and *eth* is added. Spell the numbers ending in *th* below. Use your dictionary if you are not sure of a spelling.

1. 4th ___fourth___
2. 5th ___fifth___
3. 8th ___eighth___
4. 9th ___ninth___
5. 12th ___twelfth___
6. 30th ___thirtieth___
7. 40th ___fortieth___
8. 90th ___ninetieth___

5 Using the Apostrophe to Form Plurals. Add *'s* to form the plurals of letters used as words and of abbreviations with periods. Study the examples below. Then write the sentences that you hear.

p's and q's x's and o's lb.'s jr.'s V.I.P.'s I.Q.'s

1. The ship sent two SOS's.
2. Do the twins know their ABC's?
3. Remember to dot your i's and cross your t's.
4. The medical students will be M.D.'s soon.
5. Mrs. Smith belongs to three P.T.A.'s.

Lesson 8 39

3 Words That Sound Almost Alike

This exercise gives students an opportunity to consider the spelling of two pairs of words that are pronounced almost alike. In some regions of the country, these pairs are pronounced as homonyms. Students should use the dictionary if they are unsure of the correct choice in any context.

4 Numbers That End in *th*

This exercise draws students' attention to the fact that *th* is added to most numbers to indicate order or position in a series. Sometimes the spelling of the root number changes when *th* is added. Point out to students that the roots that end in *y* follow the *y* to *i* pattern and that they can hear the *e* in the *eth* ending.

If students have trouble spelling these numbers, go over the changes with them. Point out particularly that the *e* is dropped from *nine* in *ninth* but not in *ninety* and *ninetieth*, and the *u* is dropped from *four* in *forty* and *fortieth* but not in *fourth*.

5 Using the Apostrophe to Form Plurals

Adding *'s* to letters and abbreviations should not be difficult for students. It is simply a convention that should be brought to their attention. Before beginning the dictation, tell students that the sentences contain letters and abbreviations other than the examples given in the text.

6 Review of Contractions. When we put two words together and leave out one or more letters, we have a contraction. We put an apostrophe in place of the letter or letters we leave out. Study the example and then form the contractions below.

Example: are + not = aren't

1. we + are	we're	6. it + is	it's
2. is + not	isn't	7. will + not	won't
3. have + not	haven't	8. I + am	I'm
4. should + not	shouldn't	9. could + have	could've
5. he + will	he'll	10. they + are	they're

7 Homonyms: *Their, There,* and *They're*

Their is a possessive pronoun. It is used to indicate *something that belongs to them.*

There means *in that place.* It answers the question *where* and contains the word *here.*

They're is the contraction for *they are.* Use it only when you can substitute *they are* in the sentence.

Study the example sentences and then fill in the correct word to complete each of the sentences below.

Examples: This is *their* house.
Put the box *there.*
They're all going with us.
Their car is red.
There were six letters in the mail.
Do you know when *they're* coming?

1. Their cat is in the tree.
2. They're going to the party, aren't they?
3. I am going over there after school.
4. It's their decision.
5. There isn't any reason to be upset.
6. They're going to have twins.

40 Lesson 8

6 Review of Contractions

This exercise reviews the use of the apostrophe to form contractions. Contractions were introduced in Book 1 of this series. If students have difficulty with this exercise, help them to determine which letters are left out to form each contraction. Give them more practice with different contractions, if necessary.

7 Homonyms: *Their, There,* and *They're*

This exercise deals with the homonyms *their, there,* and *they're.* Go over the meaning of each word. Point out that all three of these words start with the word *the.* This often helps students who have the tendency to write *thier* instead of *their.*

Have students complete the exercise on their own. Then check to be sure they have capitalized their answers to numbers 1, 2, 5, and 6.

8 Writing a Letter. Write a letter to a friend telling about something that has happened to you recently or something you are planning to do soon. Begin with the date in the upper right corner. Use at least five words that contain *th* or *wh*.

Dear ______,

Sincerely,

9 Writing Sentences. On the lines below, write the sentences that you hear.

1. Do you know whose whistle is over there?
2. Whoever thinks he knows where to go should say so.
3. Grandmother told them to mind their p's and q's.
4. Thomas thought he could wear his brother's suit.
5. I don't know whether the weather will change in time.

Lesson 8 41

8 Writing a Letter

In this exercise students use a letter as the format for free writing.

Encourage students to write freely and to use additional paper if necessary. Be sure they understand where the date should be placed. Mark only the spellings of words for which you feel they should definitely be held responsible.

9 Writing Sentences

Instruct students to write the sentences that you dictate, which are on the replica of the student page.

These sentences give students an opportunity to write the sight words and some of the representative words in context. Note any specific errors that students make, and design additional words, sentences, or phrases for specific problems.

In addition to the blends covered in this lesson, the patterns found in these sentences include:
—homonyms (1 and 3)
—almost homonyms (2, 4, and 5)
—contractions (5)
—apostrophe to form plural (3)
—possessive pronouns (3 and 4)
—possessives (4)

Review of Unit 2

Digraphs and Suffixes

1 Words That End in /shən/. Write three of the ways to spell /shən/ at the end of words.

tion ____ sion ____ cian ____

Fill in the correct spelling of /shən/ to complete each of the words below.

1. ambi tion	5. ses sion	9. magi cian
2. admis sion	6. sta tion	10. transporta tion
3. infla tion	7. vaca tion	11. conversa tion
4. opti cian	8. dona tion	12. occupa tion

What is the most common way to spell /shən/ at the end of a word? tion

What is the ending that indicates a person skilled in some work? cian

Write two sight words that end in *shion*.

fashion ____ cushion ____

2 Words That End in /chur/. Write the words that you hear.

1. lecture	3. teacher	5. richer
2. feature	4. mixture	6. adventure

How is the sound /chur/ usually spelled at the end of words? ture

3 Homonyms. Use each of these homonyms correctly in a sentence.

1. their ____
2. there ____
3. they're ____

Review of Unit 2

Digraphs and Suffixes

Objectives

- **Suffixes:** Review three spellings for /shən/ and patterns for predicting the correct spelling. Complete words by filling in the correct spelling of /shən/.
- **Alternative Spellings:** Review alternative spellings for /chur/.
- **Homonyms:** Review designated homonyms by using them in original sentences.
- **Using Apostrophes:** Review various uses of the apostrophe.
- **Root Words:** Identify root words of words that end in /shən/.
- **Writing Sentences:** Practice writing representative and sight words in context.
- **Composing Sentences:** Write original sentences using representative and sight words.
- **Puzzle:** Review representative words and sight words by completing a crossword puzzle.

1 Words That End in /shən/

This exercise reviews the suffixes *-tion*, *-sion*, and *-cian* and the fact that *-tion* is the most common spelling for /shən/ as an ending. Explain that each of the given words ends in the sound /shən/, so students should say the whole word to themselves before determining which way the suffix is spelled.

2 Words That End in /chur/

This exercise reviews the alternative spellings of /chur/ at the end of words. Remind students before they begin that /chur/ can be spelled *ture* or *cher* and that *ture* is the more common spelling.

3 Homonyms

This exercise requires students to use homonyms correctly rather than recognize their correct use. Encourage students to use their dictionaries if necessary.

4 Review of the Apostrophe. Rewrite the phrases and sentences below filling in the missing apostrophes.

1. Jims transfer — Jim's transfer
2. Mind your ps and qs. — Mind your p's and q's.
3. the childrens father — the children's father
4. Its not necessary. — It's not necessary.
5. Theyre all musicians. — They're all musicians.
6. Youve got my permission. — You've got my permission.

5 Finding Root Words. Write the root word for each of the words below. Use the dictionary to check your spelling if necessary.

1. admission — admit
2. celebration — celebrate
3. confession — confess
4. combination — combine
5. beautician — beauty
6. occupation — occupy
7. communication — communicate
8. confusion — confuse
9. imagination — imagine
10. electrician — electric
11. suspension — suspend
12. satisfaction — satisfy

6 Writing Sentences. Write the sentences that you hear.

1. There was a discussion about pollution on our local television station.
2. A physician lectured about problems with chemical wastes.
3. Three politicians shared their thoughts on the problem.
4. Then people telephoned to say what they think we should do.
5. The fifth caller said we have to give nature a chance.
6. Everyone agreed that we're all in this together.

Review of Unit 2 43

4 Review of the Apostrophe

This exercise reviews the use of the apostrophe to form possessives, contractions, and the plurals of letters and abbreviations.

5 Finding Root Words

This exercise reinforces the relationship between root words and the words formed from them. When going over this exercise, have students note the various ways in which the spellings of the root words change when the suffixes are added.

6 Writing Sentences

Instruct students to write the sentences that you dictate, which are on the replica of the student page.

These sentences give students an opportunity to write some of the sight words and representative words from this unit in context. Note any specific errors that students make, and design additional words, sentences, or phrases for specific problems.

In addition to the blends covered in this unit, the patterns found in these sentences include:

—words ending in /shən/ (1, 2, and 3)
—homonyms (1 and 3)
—Silent *e* Pattern 1 (2, 3, and 4)
—words ending in /chur/ (2 and 5)
—possessive pronouns (1 and 3)
—numbers with *th* (5)
—contractions (6)

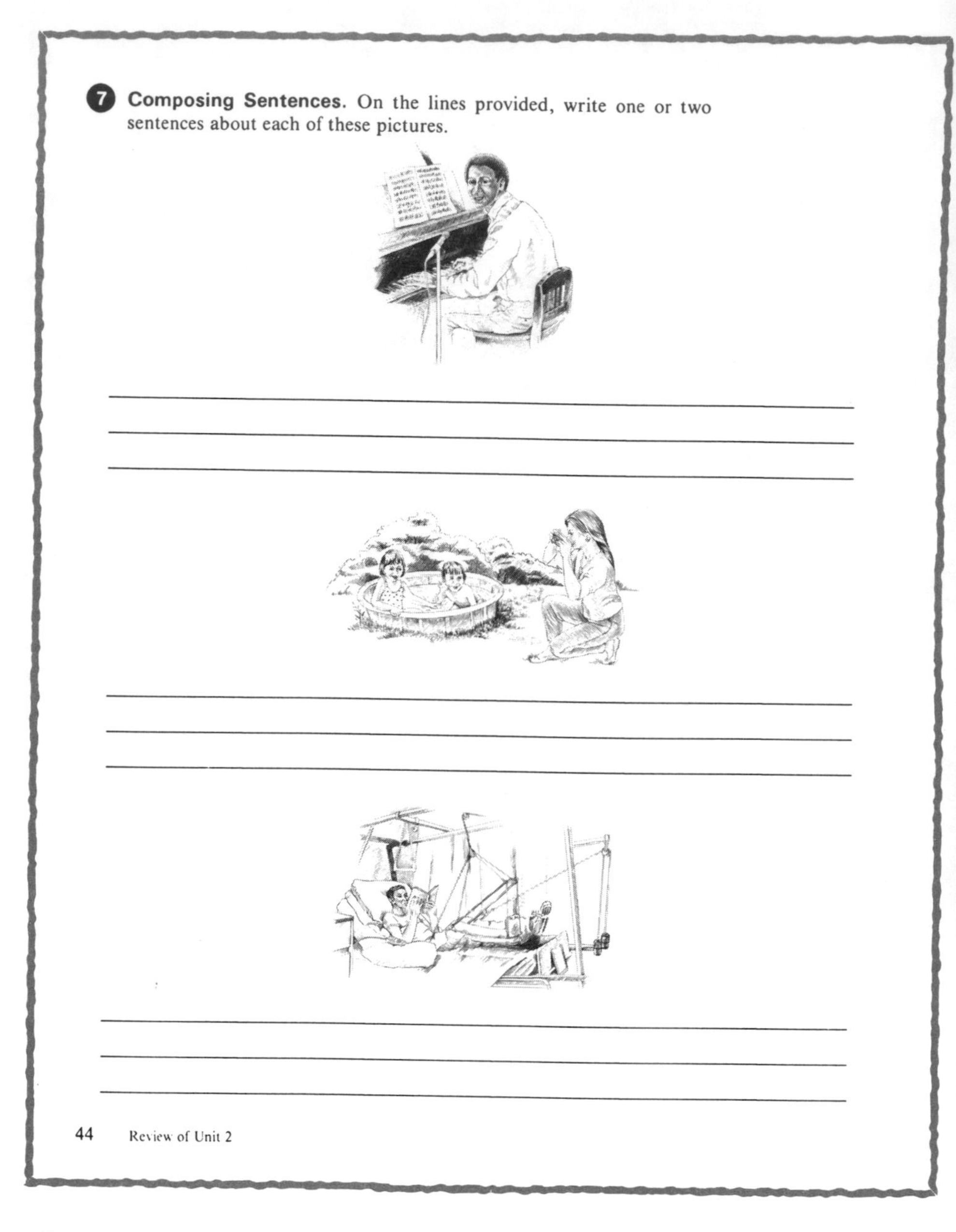

7 Composing Sentences. On the lines provided, write one or two sentences about each of these pictures.

44 Review of Unit 2

7 Composing Sentences

This exercise provides an opportunity for students to do some free writing. It is important for them to recognize that their spelling has improved and that this, in turn, has resulted in more fluent writing.

Discuss the illustrations briefly before students begin to write. Encourage them to use words they have learned how to spell in this book. Suggest that they use the word lists at the back of the book for ideas. Also encourage them to look up words they aren't sure of after they have finished writing.

Remember that errors in words that haven't been studied yet shouldn't be treated negatively. Point out any parts of the word that are spelled correctly and praise the effort. This exercise is intended to provide positive reinforcement for students, so it is important to emphasize the correctly spelled portions of misspelled words.

8 Crossword Puzzle. Use the clues below to complete this crossword puzzle. Most of the answers are representative words or sight words from Unit 2 or contain Unit 2 digraphs or endings.

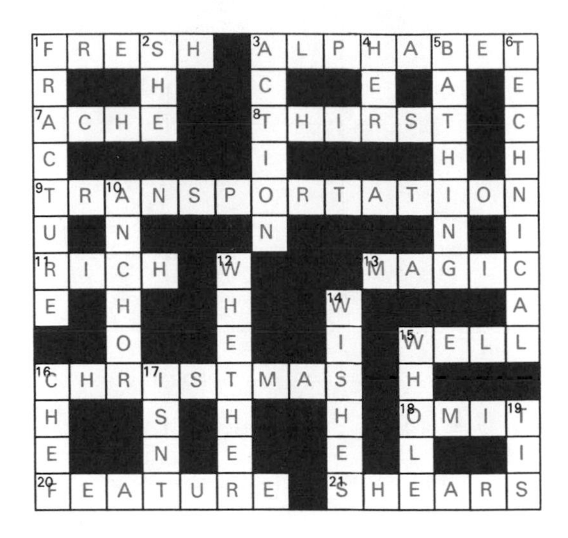

Across

1. The opposite of stale
3. The ABC's
7. Pain
8. A need for water
9. A system of traveling
11. The opposite of poor
13. What a magician performs
15. The opposite of ill
16. December 25
18. Leave out
20. A characteristic or quality
21. Large scissors

Down

1. To break, as a bone
2. The opposite of he
3. A movement, act, or deed
4. The opposite of his: ___ book
5. Taking a bath
6. Related to mechanical or industrial skills
10. This holds a boat in place.
12. Almost a homonym of weather
14. Wants or desires: He ___ he could go with us.
15. Complete; entire
16. A French cook
17. The contraction for *is not*
19. A contraction for *it is*: "My Country ___ of Thee"

Review of Unit 2 45

8 Crossword Puzzle

Have students complete the crossword puzzle. Tell them that most of the answer words are representative or sight words from Unit 2. The clues are mostly definitions that rely on the students' general knowledge.

Allow them to use a dictionary if they want to. You might want them to work in pairs or small groups. If necessary, give them the following list of answer words and have them check off words as they use them.

ache	omit
action	rich
alphabet	she
anchor	shears
bathing	technical
chef	thirst
Christmas	'tis
feature	transportation
fracture	whether
fresh	whole
her	well
isn't	wishes
magic	

Unit 2 Tests

We recommend that you test your students on the representative words and sight words from Unit 2 before going on. The following are suggested lists of representative words and sight words from Unit 2. You may want to substitute other words to meet the needs of your students.

Dictate each word and use it in a simple sentence. Students should be able to spell 90 percent of the representative words and 13 of the 15 sight words correctly.

Representative Words	Sight Words
1. flesh	1. sure
2. anything	2. whose
3. ache	3. ocean
4. phone	4. fashion
5. addition	5. suspicion
6. bleach	6. sugar
7. admission	7. cushion
8. picture	8. psychology
9. truth	9. machine
10. awhile	10. whoever
11. musician	11. spatula
12. though	12. natural
13. television	13. wear
14. chain	14. weather
15. where	15. thought
16. shoulder	
17. stomach	
18. adventure	
19. vacation	
20. alphabet	

Lesson 9

The Blends *str*, *scr*, *spl*, and *spr*

Objectives

- **Blends:** Learn to spell words with the blends *str*, *scr*, *spl*, and *spr*.
- **Sight Words:** Learn to spell *straight*, *strength*, and *spread*.
- **Word Building:** Write the missing syllables of dictated words.
- **Composing Sentences:** Write original sentences using selected words.
- **Endings:** Add endings to words following Doubling Pattern 2.
- **Patterns:** Review six patterns for adding endings. Learn to apply Doubling Pattern 2 to words that end in *-fer*.
- **Root Words:** Identify the root words of designated words and the pattern that was followed to form each word.
- **Writing Sentences:** Practice writing representative and sight words in context.

Sight Words

Teach the sight words using the methods described on pages 9-12 in the introduction to this book.

All these sight words contain blends presented in this lesson. Point out to students the *ea* spelling of /ĕ/ in *spread* and ask them what sound *ea* usually spells. Review *weather*, a Lesson 8 sight word, in which /ĕ/ is also spelled *ea*. This spelling of /ĕ/ will be covered in Book 4 of this series. If students have difficulty with the spelling of *spread*, suggest that they make a mental picture of the spelling of the word.

Lesson 9

The Blends *str*, *scr*, *spl*, and *spr*

Sight Words		
straight	strength	spread

Blends

❶ Listening

str — Listen to the sound of *str* in these words.

strap	strike	stream
string	struck	street
strong	stretch	strange

scr — Listen to the sound of *scr* in these words.

scrap	scrape	describe
scrub	scream	description
scratch	screen	inscription

spl — Listen to the sound of *spl* in these words.

split	splice	splatter
splash	splinter	splendid

spr — Listen to the sound of *spr* in these words.

spray	spring	spry
sprain	sprinkle	spree

❷ Writing Words. On the lines below, write the words that you hear.

1. sprung	5. stroke	9. sprinkle
2. stretch	6. strap	10. splinter
3. scream	7. inscribe	11. description
4. splitting	8. splendid	12. springtime

46 Lesson 9

❶ Listening

Explain to students that all the blends in this lesson have three letters. Point out that all three letters can be heard in each blend.

Introduce the words with the blend *str* using the following steps.

1. Say the sound /str/ and ask students what letters make the sound.
2. Say the letters *s-t-r* and ask students what sound they make.
3. Say the word *strap* and ask students what letters spell /str/ and what letters spell /ap/.
4. Say the word *strap* and ask students what letters spell *strap*.

Follow the same steps to introduce the words with the blends *scr*, *spl*, and *spr*.

Make sure that students know the meanings of all the representative words before going on with the lesson.

❷ Writing Words

Instruct students to write the words that you dictate, which are found on the replica of the student page. Say each word, use it in a phrase or simple sentence, and say the word again.

3 Word Building. Listen to the dictated words and fill in the missing syllable to complete each word below.

1. struc ture	5. pre scrip tion
2. scrib ble	6. strat e gy
3. splut ter	7. un scru pu lous
4. splen dor	8. in de struc ti ble

Use two of these words in sentences. Look up the words in your dictionary if you need to.

1. ____________________

____

2. ____________________

____

4 Review of Doubling Pattern 2. Review the pattern and follow the directions below.

Pattern: In words of two or more syllables, double the final consonant only when:

- the last syllable has one vowel and one final consonant
- the last syllable is the accented syllable
- and the ending starts with a vowel.

Add the endings to the words below. Double the final consonant when necessary.

1. admit + ing	admitting	7. splatter + ed	splattered
2. splinter + ing	splintering	8. begin + ing	beginning
3. propel + er	propeller	9. forget + ing	forgetting
4. omit + ing	omitting	10. splendid + ly	splendidly
5. inspect + or	inspector	11. transmit + er	transmitter
6. forbid + en	forbidden	12. prosper + ous	prosperous

Lesson 9 47

3 Word Building

This exercise requires students to isolate and spell single syllables. Dictate the entire word, giving students time to isolate the missing syllable and write it in the blank.

Notice that two lines are allowed for each of the sentences students will write. Encourage them to write fairly lengthy sentences. You might challenge them to use several of the representative words in Exercise 1 in each sentence.

4 Review of Doubling Pattern 2

This exercise reviews the doubling pattern introduced in Lesson 3. If students have difficulty with any aspect of this, review the procedures used to teach it in Lesson 3 and provide appropriate reinforcement exercises.

Some students will continue to have difficulty identifying the accented syllable. Work with these students individually, emphasizing the accented syllable as you pronounce a word for them.

5 **Reviewing Patterns for Adding Endings.** Review these patterns for adding endings.

1. **Doubling Pattern 1.** Double the final consonant if the word has one syllable, one vowel, and one final consonant, and the ending begins with a vowel. Do not double *w* or *x*.
2. **Doubling Pattern 2.** In words of more than one syllable, the final consonant is doubled if the last syllable is accented and has one vowel and one final consonant, and if the ending starts with a vowel.
3. **Silent *e* Pattern 1.** Drop the final silent *e* if the ending begins with a vowel.
4. **The Ending *-es*.** When a word ends in *s*, *x*, *z*, *ch*, or *sh*, add *-es* instead of *-s*.
5. **Changing *y* to *i*.** When adding an ending to a word that ends in Cy, change the *y* to *i* unless the ending begins with *i*. Add *-es* instead of *-s* to nouns and verbs.
6. **Changing *f* to *v*.** The plural of some words which end in *f* or *fe* is formed by changing the *f* or *fe* to *v* and adding *-es*.

Write the root word for each of the words listed below. Then write the number of the pattern which was followed when the ending was added. The first one has been done to get you started.

	Root Word	Pattern
1. scrubbed	scrub	1
2. describing	describe	3
3. propeller	propel	2
4. shadier	shady	5
5. stretches	stretch	4
6. shelves	shelf	6
7. stranger	strange	3
8. splitting	split	1
9. glasses	glass	4
10. forgotten	forgot	2

48 Lesson 9

5 Reviewing Patterns for Adding Endings

This exercise reviews the major patterns for adding endings that students have studied so far in this series. Go over the six patterns with the students, and then have them complete the exercise on their own.

When they remove endings to find the root words, students become aware of spelling changes that occur when some of these words are formed.

6 Words That End in *-fer*. When Doubling Pattern 2 is used with words that end in *-fer*, it is more difficult to decide whether or not to double the final *r*. This is because the accent sometimes changes to a different syllable when the ending is added.

Part A. Pronounce the words below and mark the accented syllable with an accent mark (′).

1. re fer′   re fer′ ral   ref′ er ence
2. con fer′   con fer′ ring   con′ fer ence

Underline the words in which the *r* was doubled and fill in the blanks below.

1. The *r* is doubled if the accent stays on the ___second___ syllable when the ending is added.
2. The *r* is not doubled if the accent shifts to the ___first___ syllable when the ending is added.

Part B. Add the endings to the words below. Remember to pronounce the word with the ending added to determine which syllable is accented. Use the dictionary if necessary.

1. prefer + ed ___preferred___
2. prefer + able ___preferable___
3. prefer + ence ___preference___
4. prefer + ing ___preferring___
5. offer + ed ___offered___
6. infer + ing ___inferring___
7. infer + ence ___inference___
8. differ + ence ___difference___
9. differ + ed ___differed___
10. refer + ee ___referee___

7 Writing Sentences. On the lines below, write the sentences that you hear.

1. Fran has a splitting headache.
2. This stretch of road is very straight.
3. Chris struck the ball with all her strength.
4. The smoke spread to the houses across the street.
5. Steve gave us a description of the picture he preferred.

Lesson 9 49

6 Words That End in *-fer*

Words that end in *-fer* can be troublesome for students because the accent sometimes shifts to a different syllable when an ending is added. Emphasize that students must pronounce the word aloud with the ending added and determine which syllable is accented. If the accent stays on *-fer*, then the *r* is doubled. If the accent shifts to the first syllable when the ending is added, the *r* is not doubled.

In Part A of the exercise, students discover this pattern. In Part B, students apply this information to words that end in *-fer*.

Additional Activity:

You may want to point out to students who can benefit from the information that words that end in *-fer* take the endings *-ence*, *-ent*, and *-ency* rather than *-ance*, *-ant*, and *-ancy*.

7 Writing Sentences

Instruct students to write the sentences that you dictate, which are on the replica of the student page.

These sentences give students an opportunity to write the sight words and some of the representative words in context. Note any specific errors that students make, and design additional words, sentences, or phrases for specific problems.

In addition to the blends covered in this lesson, the patterns found in these sentences include:
—Doubling Pattern 1 (1)
—Compound words (1)
—Doubling Pattern 2 (5)
—words ending in /shən/ (5)
—words ending in /chur/ (5)

Lesson 10

The Blends *squ*, *shr*, and *thr*

Objectives

- **Blends:** Learn to spell words with the blends *squ*, *shr*, and *thr*.
- **Sight Words:** Learn to spell *squirrel*, *shriek*, *shrewd*, and *thread.*
- **Dictionary Skills:** Review the use of guide words to determine where to find words in the dictionary.
- **Writing by Syllables:** Write dictated words one syllable at a time.
- **Composing Sentences:** Write original sentences using selected and designated words.
- **Homonyms:** Learn to distinguish between *threw* and *through.*
- **Pattern:** Review the *y* to *i* pattern and use it to add endings to words. Practice the *y* to *i* pattern by writing dictated phrases.
- **Writing Sentences:** Practice writing representative words and sight words in context.
- **Puzzle:** Use representative and sight words to complete a puzzle.

Sight Words

Teach the sight words using the methods described on pages 9-12 in the introduction to this book. These sight words contain the blends presented in this lesson.

The vowel combination *ew* in *shrewd* may be particularly difficult for some students. You might suggest that students make a mental picture of the spelling of this word.

Point out *ea* spells /ĕ/ in *thread.* Remind students of the same pattern in *weather* and *spread*, sight words in Lessons 8 and 9.

Lesson 10

The Blends *squ*, *shr*, and *thr*

Sight Words			
squirrel	shriek	shrewd	thread

Blends

❶ Listening

squ

Listen to the sound of *squ* in these words.

square	squad	squeeze
squeak	squat	squander
squeal	squall	squeamish

shr

Listen to the sound of *shr* in these words.

shred	shrink	shrimp
shrub	shrank	shrine
shrill	shrunk	shrivel

thr

Listen to the sound of *thr* in these words.

thrill	throw	three
throng	threw	thrive
thrust	through	throat

❷ Writing Words. On the lines below, write the words that you hear.

1. shred
2. throw
3. square
4. shrill
5. thriving
6. squatting
7. throat
8. shrug
9. squeamish

50 Lesson 10

---

❶ Listening

Remind students that *q* is followed by *u* in English words and that *qu* makes the sound /kw/.

Introduce the words with the blend *squ* using the following steps.

1. Say the sound /skw/ and ask students what letters make the sound.
2. Say the letters *s-q-u* and ask students what sound they make.
3. Say the word *square* and ask students what letters spell /skw/ and what letters spell /âr/.
4. Say the word *square* and ask students what letters spell *square.*

Follow the same steps to introduce the words with the blends *shr* and *thr.*

Draw attention to the *ew* in *threw.* Point out that this is the same spelling that was in the sight word *shrewd.* If necessary, treat *threw* as a sight word also.

Draw attention to other patterns students have studied, such as /ē/ spelled *ea* and *ee*; the double *l* in *squall*, *shrill*, and *thrill*, and so forth.

Make sure that students know the meanings of all the representative words before going on with the lesson.

3 Dictionary Skills: Guide Words. Below are pairs of guide words that might be found on dictionary pages. Decide if the words listed below each pair would appear on the dictionary page that has those guide words. Underline each word that would be found on that page.

1. **square — squeal**
   squad squash squeak squall
2. **shred — shrink**
   shrill shrank shrimp shrewd
3. **three — thrive**
   thread threw thrill threat
4. **squander — squeeze**
   squeamish squirrel squadron squat
5. **shrivel — shrunk**
   shriek shrub shrug shrive
6. **throw — thrust**
   through throat throng thrush

4 Writing Words by Syllables. Write each word your teacher dictates by syllables. Then write the whole word on the line provided.

	First Syllable	Second Syllable	Third Syllable	Fourth Syllable	Whole Word
1.	scrib	ble			scribble
2.	in	crease			increase
3.	sub	scribe			subscribe
4.	sub	sti	tute		substitute
5.	nu	tri	tion		nutrition
6.	con	grat	u	late	congratulate
7.	con	sti	tu	tion	constitution
8.	con	cen	tra	tion	concentration

Use two of the words above in sentences.

1. ______________________________
2. ______________________________

Lesson 10 51

2 Writing Words

Instruct students to write the words that you dictate, which are found on the replica of the student page. Say each word, use it in a phrase or simple sentence, and say the word again.

3 Dictionary Skills: Guide Words

Remind students that the guide words at the top of a dictionary page are the first and last entry words on that page. Make sure students understand that any word on that page must come alphabetically after the first guide word and before the second guide word.

Since all of these words begin with three-letter blends, students will have to compare the fourth or fifth letters of the entry word and the guide words to determine which words would appear on the dictionary page. You may want to do the first one or two items together as a group.

One technique for teaching the use of guide words is to have students cover up common letters in the entry word and the guide words and then determine if the remaining letter(s) fit between the guide words.

4 Writing Words by Syllables

Dictate the words by syllables, emphasizing the syllables. Then pronounce the whole word normally. Remind students that the number of blanks indicates the number of syllables in the word.

These words contain some of the blends students have been studying. Help them to predict the spelling of these words.

Pay particular attention to the following words.

1. *Congratulate*: Point out that /chū/ is spelled *tu* as it is in words ending in *ture*.
2. *Substitute* and *constitution*: Point out the *sti* syllable in each of these words.

Don't worry about formal syllable divisions. Emphasize the division students hear. It is more important for them to spell the word correctly than to have their syllabication match that of the dictionary.

Additional Activities:

Have students look up the meanings of any of these words that they don't already know.

Have them use the rest of the words in original sentences.

5 **Homonyms: *Threw* and *Through*.** *Threw* is the past tense of *throw*. Study the examples below to see several ways that *through* is used.

1. We wandered *through* the shopping mall.
2. It rained all *through* the afternoon.
3. Are you *through* with that assignment?
4. He *threw* the ball *through* the window.

Use each of these homonyms in a sentence of your own.

threw ______________________________

____

through ______________________________

____

6 **Review of Changing *y* to *i*.** When adding an ending to a word that ends in a consonant plus *y*, change the *y* to *i* unless the ending begins with *i*. Add *-es* instead of *-s* to nouns and verbs.

Part A. Add the endings to these words.

1. sky + es ___skies___
2. crazy + ly ___crazily___
3. squeaky + est ___squeakiest___
4. library + es ___libraries___
5. thirty + eth ___thirtieth___
6. century + es ___centuries___
7. cry + ing ___crying___
8. thirsty + er ___thirstier___
9. technology + es ___technologies___
10. pretty + est ___prettiest___
11. study + ing ___studying___
12. tragedy + es ___tragedies___

Part B. Write the phrases you hear.

1. ___three countries___
2. ___the prettiest shrubs___
3. ___the squeakiest wheel___
4. ___studying writing___
5. ___the twentieth century___
6. ___the shadiest lanes___
7. ___tried to win___
8. ___flying to Spain___
9. ___beautiful scene___
10. ___shrill cries___

52 Lesson 10

5 Homonyms: *Threw* and *Through*

Encourage students to write fairly lengthy sentences using these homonyms or to write two sentences for each word.

6 Review of Changing *y* to *i*

This exercise reviews a pattern introduced in Book 2. When a word ends in **C**y, we change the *y* to *i* before adding a suffix unless the suffix begins with *i*. When making nouns plural, we change the *y* to *i* and add *es*. The third person singular of the present tense of verbs that end in **C**y is also formed by changing *y* to *i* and adding *-es* (I *fly*, it *flies*).

Before students begin Part A, emphasize that, when adding an ending to a word that ends in **C**y, the *y* is always changed to *i* unless the suffix begins with *i*.

The phrases in Part B give students an opportunity to practice this pattern with words in context. You may want to remind students that, since these are phrases, they should not be capitalized or punctuated like sentences.

7 Writing Sentences. On the lines below, write the sentences that you hear.

1. Fred made a very shrewd decision.
2. The children threw nuts to the squirrels.
3. That wheel is getting squeakier all the time.
4. The kids ran shrieking through the sprinkler's spray.
5. If you pull on that thread, the whole hem will come out.

8 Puzzle. Use the clues at the left to fill in the blocks of the puzzle. Refer to the list of answer words at the bottom of the page if you need to. When all the correct answers are filled in, the shaded blocks will spell a new word that begins with a blend.

Clues

1. used with a needle for sewing — T H R E A D
2. to make smaller — S H R I N K
3. a small tree-climbing rodent — S Q U I R R E L
4. to press firmly; to hug — S Q U E E Z E
5. a rectangle with four equal sides — S Q U A R E
6. a small, edible shellfish — S H R I M P
7. to hurl or fling through the air — T H R O W
8. to shrink and wrinkle — S H R I V E L
9. a team of people — S Q U A D

The new word: THRESHOLD

Write a sentence using the new word.

Word List: shrimp, shrink, shrivel, squad, square, squeeze, squirrel, thread, throw

Lesson 10 53

7 Writing Sentences

Instruct students to write the sentences that you dictate, which are on the replica of the student page.

These sentences give students an opportunity to write the sight words and some of the representative words in context. Note any specific errors that students make, and design additional words, sentences, or phrases for specific problems.

In addition to the blends covered in this lesson, the patterns found in these sentences include:
—words ending in /shən/ (1)
—Doubling Pattern 1 (3)
—changing *y* to *i* (3)
—possessives (4)

8 Puzzle

Have students complete the puzzle by writing each answer word in the blocks next to the clue. An alphabetized list of answers is provided at the bottom of the page.

When students have completed the puzzle, the word *threshold* will be spelled vertically in the shaded blocks. Have students write this word on the line provided and use it in an original sentence. Have them look it up in their dictionaries if they are not sure of its meaning.

Review of Unit 3

Beginning Blends of Three Letters

1 Word Building. Add one of the beginning blends below to each word family to make a word. Do not make the same word twice.

str scr spl spr squ shr thr

1. str ap	6. str eam	11. thr ill
2. spr ay	7. shr ed	12. shr ill
3. str ay	8. squ eeze	13. spr ing
4. squ eak	9. spl ice	14. thr ong
5. scr eam	10. str ike	15. scr ub

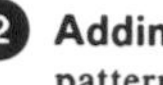

Adding Endings. Add the endings to the words below following the patterns you have studied.

1. split + ing	splitting	11. reply + s *or* es	replies
2. thirsty + er	thirstier	12. scatter + ing	scattering
3. inspect + or	inspector	13. squat + er	squatter
4. thrive + ing	thriving	14. bleach + s *or* es	bleaches
5. shelf + s *or* es	shelves	15. fly + ing	flying
6. shop + ing	shopping	16. scratch + s *or* es	scratches
7. scrub + er	scrubber	17. strike + ing	striking
8. refer + ed	referred	18. commit + ee	committee
9. fifty + eth	fiftieth	19. lecture + ing	lecturing
10. permit + ing	permitting	20. century + s *or* es	centuries

54 Review of Unit 3

Review of Unit 3

Beginning Blends of Three Letters

Objectives

- **Word Building:** Add three-letter initial blends to short- and long-vowel word families.
- **Endings:** Add designated endings to words following various patterns.
- **Polysyllabic Words:** Use polysyllabic words to complete sentences.
- **Composing Sentences:** Write original sentences using selected words.
- **Composing Paragraphs:** Write an original paragraph using representative and sight words.
- **Writing Sentences:** Practice writing representative and sight words in context.
- **Puzzle:** Review representative and sight words by completing a crossword puzzle.

1 Word Building

Have students add one of the beginning blends to each word family to make a word. Encourage them to use all of the blends at least once. The answers given on the replica of the student page are examples. Accept all correctly spelled words.

2 Adding Endings

This exercise reviews the various patterns students have studied for adding endings to words. If students have had trouble with any of these, you may want to review the patterns listed in Exercise 5 of Lesson 9 before they begin this review.

Additional Activity:

Have students identify the pattern they followed for each word they formed in the exercise. Remind them that if nothing in the root word changes when the ending is added, that is the regular pattern.

3 Using Words with Many Syllables. Fill in the blanks in the sentences with the words listed below. Use each word only once.

concentration	conversation	expression	responsible
congratulate	especially	illustrations	spectacular
Constitution	explanation	nutrition	substitute

1. Good health depends on good nutrition.
2. I want to congratulate you on your success.
3. Did Steve give you an explanation for his absence?
4. The Fourth of July fireworks were spectacular.
5. The three men were having a very lively conversation.
6. Shirley is not especially fond of that type of music.
7. Do you know who was responsible for the accident?
8. If you can't attend the meeting, will you send a substitute?
9. The speaker gave several illustrations to explain his point of view.
10. The subject Clint is studying requires a great deal of concentration
11. The Supreme Court interprets the Constitution of the United States.
12. You should have seen the expression on Chris's face when we walked in.

4 Composing Sentences. Choose three of the words listed in Exercise 3 and use them in sentences of your own.

1. ____________________
2. ____________________
3. ____________________

Review of Unit 3 55

3 Using Words with Many Syllables

In this exercise, students have the opportunity to use in context several of the polysyllabic words that they have written by syllables in earlier lessons. Encourage them to use their dictionaries if they want to.

4 Composing Sentences

When students are writing original sentences, encourage them to attempt to spell words they haven't studied. Encourage them also to look up words they aren't sure of when they have finished writing. Praise linguistically reasonable attempts, even if they are not the actual spellings.

5 Composing a Paragraph. On a separate sheet of paper, write a paragraph of three or four sentences about this scene. Use some of the words listed below in your sentences.

scream	sprain	stretch	throat
shriek	squad	threw	throng
shrill	strength	thrill	throw

TIME 0:03 HOME 88 VISITORS 88

6 Writing Sentences. On the lines below, write the sentences that you hear.

1. Can you squeeze through that opening?
2. The pitcher threw three strikes in a row.
3. My jeans have shrunk so much I can't squat in them.
4. The dog splashed in the pond and had a splendid time.
5. Right after I sprayed the grass, it began to sprinkle.
6. A strange inscription had been scratched into the stone.

56 Review of Unit 3

5 Composing a Paragraph

Discuss the illustration with students before they begin to write. Encourage them to use as many representative words and sight words from this unit as they can.

Encourage students to look up words they aren't sure of after they have finished writing. Remember that errors in words that haven't been studied yet shouldn't be treated negatively. Point out any parts of the word that are spelled correctly and praise the effort.

6 Writing Sentences

Instruct students to write the sentences that you dictate, which are on the replica of the student page.

These sentences give students an opportunity to write some of the sight words and representative words from this unit in context. Note any specific errors that students make, and design additional words, sentences, or phrases for specific problems.

In addition to the blends covered in this unit, the patterns found in these sentences include:
—homonyms (1 and 2)
—words ending in /chur/ (2)
—contractions (3)
—words ending in /shən/ (6)

7 Crossword Puzzle. Use the clues below to complete this crossword puzzle. Most of the answers are representative words or sight words from Unit 3 or contain Unit 3 blends.

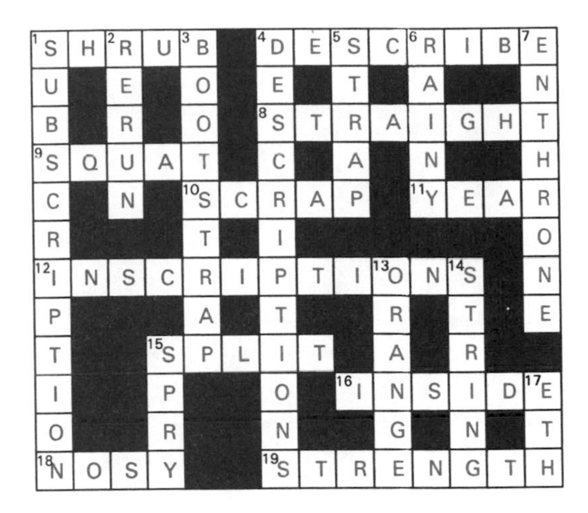

Across

1. A small plant or bush
4. To tell about
8. The opposite of crooked
9. To kneel with your weight on your heels; to crouch
10. A small piece of cloth; something left over
11. Twelve months
12. Words written or engraved on monuments
15. A favorite ice cream dish: banana ___
16. The opposite of outside
18. Snoopy; not minding your own business
19. Force or power: He has great ___.

Down

1. An order for a magazine
2. A TV program the second time it is shown
3. A strip of leather for fastening a boot
4. Words that describe
5. A thin strip used for fastening something
6. Wet weather: It was very ___.
7. To place on a throne
13. The second color in the rainbow
14. Thin cord used for tying packages
15. Quick; able to move easily
17. An ending for numbers that indicates position in a series

Review of Unit 3 57

7 Crossword Puzzle

Have students complete the crossword puzzle. Tell them that most of the answer words are representative or sight words from Unit 3. The clues are mostly definitions that rely on the students' general knowledge.

Allow them to use a dictionary if they want to. You might want them to work in pairs or small groups. If necessary, give them the following list of answer words and have them check off words as they use them.

bootstrap
describe
descriptions
enthrone
eth
inscriptions
inside
nosy
orange
rainy
rerun
scrap
shrub
split
spry
squat
straight
strap
strength
string
subscription
year

Unit 3 Tests

We recommend that you test your students on the representative words and sight words from Unit 3 before going on. The following are suggested lists of representative words and sight words from Unit 3. You may want to substitute other words to meet the needs of your students.

Dictate each word and use it in a simple sentence. Students should be able to spell 90 percent of the representative words and four of the five sight words correctly.

Representative Words

1. shrill
2. strap
3. describe
4. stretch
5. sprain
6. scrape
7. scream
8. splash
9. splendid
10. spring
11. street
12. sprinkle
13. square
14. squad
15. throat
16. shred
17. strange
18. shrub
19. splinter
20. through

Sight Words

1. straight
2. strength
3. spread
4. squirrel
5. thread

Lesson 11

The Blends *nd*, *nt*, *nce*, and *nse*

Objectives

- **Blends:** Learn to spell words with the blends *nd*, *nt*, *nce*, and *nse*.
- **Sight Words:** Learn to spell *guard*, *guardian*, *view*, *review*, *interview*, and *restaurant*.
- **Sound Discrimination:** Discriminate between words that end in *nd* and *nt*.
- **Alternative Spellings:** Learn that /ns/ at the end of words can be spelled three ways and that *nce* is the most common spelling.
- **Word Building:** Fill in *nce*, *nse*, or *nts* to spell words in context. Form nouns from verbs by adding *-ance* or *-ence*. Add prefixes and suffixes to root words.
- **Patterns:** Review Silent *e* Pattern 1. Discover the first part of Silent *e* Pattern 2.
- **Endings:** Add endings to words that end in *ce* following Silent *e* Pattern 2.
- **Composing Sentences:** Write original sentences using selected words.
- **Writing Sentences:** Practice writing representative and sight words in context.

Sight Words

Teach the sight words using the methods described on pages 9-12 in the introduction to this book.

Point out the silent *u* in *guard* and *guardian*. Note the *ew* spelling in *view*, and point out that *review* and *interview* are built from *view*. Draw attention to the *au* in *restaurant* and suggest that students make a mental picture of the spelling of this word.

Lesson 11

The Blends *nd*, *nt*, *nce*, and *nse*

Sight Words		
guard	view	interview
guardian	review	restaurant

Blends

1 Listening

nd — Listen to the sound of *nd* in these words.

bind	bandage	defend	fond
find	handful	offend	found
remind	grandfather	pretend	respond

nt — Listen to the sound of *nt* in these words.

pint	aunt	cent	rent
faint	infant	sent	payment
complaint	important	spent	argument

nce — Listen to the sound of *nce* in these words.

dance	fence	once	since
chance	absence	ounce	convince
entrance	sentence	announce	experience
insurance	residence	pronounce	difference

nse — Listen to the sound of *nse* in these words.

rinse	defense	expense	sense
tense	offense	response	license

2 Writing Words. On the lines below, write the words that you hear.

1. aunt
2. since
3. nonsense
4. payments
5. weekend
6. pronounce
7. friend
8. license
9. experience

58 Lesson 11

---

1 Listening

Point out that all the blends in this unit come at the end of syllables and contain the letter *n*.

Introduce the words with the blend *nd* using the following steps.

1. Say the sound /nd/ and ask students what letters make the sound.
2. Say the letters *n-d* and ask students what sound they make.
3. Say the word *bind* and ask students what letters spell /bī/ and what letters spell /nd/.
4. Say the word *bind* and ask students what letters spell *bind*.

Follow the same steps to introduce the words with the blends *nt*, *nce*, and *nse*, pointing out the silent *e* in the last two blends.

Point out that *pint* has a long *i* sound. Most words ending in *int* have a short vowel.

Draw attention to the homonyms *cent* and *sent*. Most people do not confuse these two words.

Note that in *argument*, the *e* is dropped from *argue* when *ment* is added, which is an exception to Silent *e* Pattern 1.

Contrast the spellings of *since*, *sense*, and *license*. The word *license* may be particularly troublesome for stu-

3 Distinguishing Between *nd* and *nt*. Underline the word that you hear in each pair below.

1. bend — bent	4. send — sent	7. grand — grant
2. pend — pent	5. tend — tent	8. spend — spent
3. rend — rent	6. planned — plant	9. found — fount

4 Word Building: Alternative Spellings for /ns/. Words that end in the sound /ns/ can be spelled *nce, nse,* or *nts,* although *nce* is much more common than *nse.* Fill in the blanks in the sentences below with *nce, nse,* or *nts.* Use your dictionary if you need to check the spelling of any words.

1. When my car broke down, a stranger stopped and offered assista n c e.
2. Clint gained a lot of confide n c e from his public speaking course.
3. Kent will be marching in the Independe n c e Day parade.
4. The boss will cover our expe n s e s for the confere n c e.
5. My grandmother always says "Sile n c e is golden."
6. The story Grant read to the kids was all about gia n t s.
7. Brian has to renew his driver's lice n s e next month.
8. Our coach always used to say, "The best offe n s e is a good defe n s e."

5 Word Building with *-ance* and *-ence*. The suffixes *-ance* and *-ence* can be used to form nouns from verbs. Form the nouns indicated below. Remember to follow the patterns that you have studied for adding endings.

1. admit + ance	admittance	6. differ + ence	difference
2. insure + ance	insurance	7. occur + ence	occurrence
3. attend + ance	attendance	8. reside + ence	residence
4. ignore + ance	ignorance	9. prefer + ence	preference
5. apply + ance	appliance	10. interfere + ence	interference

Lesson 11 59

dents. If so, have them treat it as a sight word.

You may want to explain to students that when an ending is added to a word that ends in a blend, the syllable break may come in the middle of the blend, as in *ban dage.*

Make sure that students know the meanings of the representative words before going on with the lesson.

2 Writing Words

Instruct students to write the words that you dictate, which are found on the replica of the student page. Say each word, use it in a phrase or sentence, and say the word again.

3 Distinguishing Between *nd* and *nt*

It is difficult for some students to discriminate between the *nd* and *nt* blends. This exercise is designed to help you identify students with this difficulty.

Dictate the following list of words, instructing students to underline the one they hear in each pair found on the student page.

1. bend	4. send	7. grand
2. pent	5. tent	8. spend
3. rent	6. plant	9. found

If students have difficulty with this exercise, spend some time with them individually, helping them to hear the differences in these sounds. Dictate the words and ask students to write them. Ask them to read the list of words to you, listening carefully to their pronunciation. Model the correct sounds for them. Make up other syllable and word pairs for continued practice if necessary.

4 Word Building: Alternative Spellings for /ns/

In this exercise, students must choose between three possible spellings that produce /ns/. Point out that *nce* is a far more common spelling than *nse*. There are only about 25 common words that end in *nse*, while there are more than 350 *nce* words.

5 Word Building with *-ance* and *-ence*

Before beginning this exercise, remind students that the suffixes *-tion* and *-sion* are also used to form nouns from verbs. Make sure students know the meanings of all the words that they form.

Point out that *-ance* has been added to all of the words in the first column and that *-ence* has been added to all of the words in the second column. Since these suffixes are usually not the accented syllables, they are both generally pronounced /əns/. There is no good way to predict whether /əns/ is spelled *-ance* or *-ence*. Tell students that the only way to be sure of which spelling to use in a word that hasn't been studied is to look it up in the dictionary.

❻ **Review of Silent *e* Pattern 1.** The silent *e* at the end of a word is dropped when an ending starting with a vowel is added. Add the endings to the words below.

1. strike + ing ___striking___
2. dance + ed ___danced___
3. square + ly ___squarely___
4. license + ed ___licensed___
5. rinse + ing ___rinsing___
6. brave + ly ___bravely___
7. strange + er ___stranger___
8. entrance + ing ___entrancing___

❼ **Silent *e* Pattern 2.** Answer the questions below to discover another silent *e* pattern.

Part A: Write the words that you hear and answer the questions.

1. ___twice___ 2. ___recite___ 3. ___icy___

Do these words have a hard or soft *c*? ___a soft c___

What letters give the *c*'s that sound? ___e, i, and y___

Part B: Write the words that you hear and answer the questions.

1. ___cabin___ 2. ___scatter___ 3. ___suitcase___

Do these words have a hard or soft *c*? ___a hard c___

What letter gives the *c*'s that sound? ___a___

Part C: Look at the words below and answer the questions.

trace + ed = traced   trace + ing = tracing   trace + able = traceable

When *-ed* and *-ing* are added to *trace*, is the final *e* kept or dropped? ___dropped___

When *-able* is added to *trace*, is the final *e* kept or dropped? ___kept___

What sound would the *c* have if the silent *e* in *traceable* were dropped? ___hard___

Pattern: When an ending that begins with *a* is added to a word that ends in *ce*, the silent *e* is kept to retain the soft *c* sound.

60 Lesson 11

❻ Review of Silent *e* Pattern 1

This exercise reviews Silent *e* Pattern 1 in preparation for learning the correlative pattern, which is introduced in Exercise 7. Make sure students understand this pattern before they begin the exercise.

❼ Silent *e* Pattern 2

In this exercise, students discover that the silent *e* is not dropped when an ending that begins with *a* is added to a word that ends with *ce*. Remind students that *c* spells both /s/ and /k/. Remind them also that when *c* spells /s/, it is called a soft *c* and when it spells /k/, it is called a hard *c*.

Part A reviews the vowels that produce the soft *c*, which were introduced in Lesson 5. Dictate *twice*, *recite*, and *icy* to students and have them answer the questions that follow.

Part B draws students' attention to the fact that when *a* follows *c* a hard *c* is produced. Dictate *cabin*, *scatter*, and *suitcase*, and have students answer the questions that follow.

In Part C, students discover that when a word ends in *ce*, the silent *e* is dropped when adding an ending that starts with *e* or *i*, but the *e* is retained if the ending starts with *a*. If students have trouble answering the third question, pronounce *tracable* (/trak′ ə bəl/) for them.

In Lesson 12, Silent *e* Pattern 2 will be expanded to include words ending in *ge* and endings that start with *o*.

8 **Adding Endings to Words That End in *ce*.** Add the endings to the words below following Silent *e* Pattern 2.

1. dance + ing dancing
2. pronounce + ed pronounced
3. pronounce + able pronounceable
4. peace + able peaceable
5. convince + ing convincing
6. embrace + ing embracing
7. embrace + able embraceable
8. notice + ed noticed
9. notice + able noticeable
10. announce + er announcer

9 **Word Building.** Add the prefixes and suffixes to the root words following the patterns you have studied.

1. in + expense + ive inexpensive
2. per + form + ance performance
3. in + offense + ive inoffensive
4. en + force + able enforceable
5. in + convenient + ly inconveniently
6. in + defense + ible indefensible
7. un + convince + ing unconvincing
8. dis + appear + ance disappearance

Use three of these words in sentences.

1. ______
2. ______
3. ______

10 **Writing Sentences.** On the lines below, write the sentences that you hear.

1. Kent doesn't find rock and roll very danceable.
2. My aunt recently received her driver's license.
3. The estate was fenced and had a guard at the entrance.
4. Grant's guardian reviewed the complaints and responded.
5. Clint had an interview for a job at the new restaurant.
6. The view from Grandfather's window reminded him of home.

Lesson 11 61

8 Adding Endings to Words That End in *ce*

Be sure students understand Silent *e* Pattern 2 before they begin this exercise. Remind them that words that end in *ce* follow Silent *e* Pattern 1 when endings begin with *e*, *i*, *y*, or a consonant. Silent *e* Pattern 2 applies to adding endings that start with *a*.

Check to see that students have retained the final *e* in numbers 3, 4, 7, and 9.

9 Word Building

This exercise requires students to build words using more than two elements. In addition, they must be on the lookout for silent *e*'s that may be dropped or retained. Make sure students know the meanings of all of these words before using them in sentences.

10 Writing Sentences

Instruct students to write the sentences that you dictate, which are on the replica of the student page.

These sentences give students an opportunity to write the sight words and some of the representative words in context. Note any specific errors that students make, and design additional words, sentences, or phrases for specific problems.

In addition to the blends covered in this lesson, the patterns found in these sentences include:

—alternative spellings for /ns/ (1, 2, 3, and 4)
—contractions (1)
—Silent *e* Pattern 2 (1)
—Silent *e* Pattern 1 (2 and 3)
—possessives (2, 4, and 6)

Lesson 12

The Blends *ng*, *nk*, *nch*, and *nge*

Objectives

- **Blends:** Learn to spell words with the ending blends *ng*, *nk*, *nch*, and *nge*.
- **Sight Words:** Learn to spell *England*, *English*, *finger*, *linger*, *longer*, and *younger*.
- **Sound Discrimination:** Discriminate between words that end in *ng* and *nk*.
- **Compound Words:** Form compound words with both elements given.
- **Composing Sentences:** Write original sentences using selected words.
- **Pattern:** Discover the rest of Silent *e* Pattern 2.
- **Endings:** Add endings to words that end in *ge* following Silent *e* Pattern 2.
- **Puzzle:** Use representative and sight words to complete a puzzle.
- **Writing Sentences:** Practice writing representative and sight words in context.

Sight Words

Teach the sight words using the methods described on pages 9-12 in the introduction to this book. Point out to students that the *g* has a hard sound in all of these words. In these words, the consonant pair *ng* is not pronounced like the *ng* blend.

Lesson 12

The Blends *ng*, *nk*, *nch*, and *nge*

Sight Words		
England	finger	longer
English	linger	younger

Blends: *ng*, *nk*, *nch*, *nge*

1 Listening

Listen to the sound of *ng* in these words.

ring	young	longing	tongue
rang	wrong	nothing	hanger
rung	strongly	standing	singer

Listen to the sound of *nk* in these words.

ink	sink	shrank
bank	sank	crankcase
trunk	sunken	thankful

Listen to the sound of *nch* in these words.

bunch	ranch	inch	French
lunch	branch	pinch	wrench
munch	brunch	clinch	workbench

Listen to the sound of *nge* in these words.

hinge	orange	exchange	lunge
cringe	changeable	strangely	lounge
fringe	arrangement	angelfish	challenge

62 Lesson 12

---

1 Listening

Introduce the words with the blend *ng* using the following steps.

1. Say the sound /ng/ and ask students what letters make the sound.
2. Say the letters *n-g* and ask students what sound they make in the first group of words.
3. Say the word *ring* and ask students what letters spell /ri/ and what letters spell /ng/.
4. Say the word *ring* and ask students what letters spell *ring*.

Point out the two *ng* blends in *longing*.

Follow the same steps to introduce the words with the blends *nk*, *nch*, and *nge*, pointing out the silent *e* in *nge*, which gives the *g* the sound of /j/.

Make sure that students know the meanings of all the representative words before going on with the lesson.

2 Writing Words. On the lines below, write the words that you hear.

1. think	5. blank	9. fringes
2. inches	6. nothing	10. lunches
3. wrong	7. French	11. tongue
4. challenge	8. thankful	12. exchanges

3 Distinguishing Between *ng* and *nk*. Underline the word that you hear in each pair below.

1. brink — bring	4. hunk — hung	7. hank — hang
2. think — thing	5. rink — ring	8. sinking — singing
3. stink — sting	6. bank — bang	9. winking — winging

4 Word Building: Compound Words. Build the compound words below. All of these compounds are closed.

1. song + bird	songbird	10. lunch + room	lunchroom
2. bench + mark	benchmark	11. long + hand	longhand
3. ring + side	ringside	12. inch + worm	inchworm
4. cow + puncher	cowpuncher	13. sink + hole	sinkhole
5. French + man	Frenchman	14. paper + hanger	paperhanger
6. ginger + bread	gingerbread	15. ranch + men	ranchmen
7. gold + finch	goldfinch	16. short + change	shortchange
8. bank + book	bankbook	17. shoe + string	shoestring
9. key + punch	keypunch	18. work + bench	workbench

Use two of these words in sentences.

1. ____________________

2. ____________________

Lesson 12 63

2 Writing Words

Instruct students to write the words that you dictate, which are found on the replica of the student page. Say each word, use it in a phrase or simple sentence, and say the word again.

3 Distinguishing Between *ng* and *nk*

It is difficult for some students to discriminate between the *ng* and the *nk* blends. This exercise is designed to help you identify students with this difficulty.

Dictate the following list of words, instructing students to underline the one they hear in each pair found on the student page.

1. bring	6. bank
2. think	7. hank
3. sting	8. singing
4. hung	9. winking
5. ring	

If students have difficulty with this exercise, spend some time with them individually, helping them to hear the differences in these sounds. Dictate the words and ask students to write them. Then ask students to read the list of words to you, listening carefully to their pronunciation. Model the correct sounds for them. Make up other syllable and word pairs for continued practice, if necessary.

4 Word Building: Compound Words

This exercise provides students with a chance to see that many words can be made from words that contain the blends in this lesson. They should have no trouble building these words.

Make sure they know the meanings of all the words they build before they write their sentences.

❺ Silent *e* Pattern 2

Part A. When a *g* has the sound /g/, it is called a hard *g*. Underline the hard *g*'s in the words below.

1. again 2. sugar 3. foregone 4. goodness

What letters follow the *g*'s to give them a hard sound? a and o

Part B. When a *g* has the sound /j/, it is called a soft *g*. Words that end in *ge* have the soft *g* sound. Underline the soft *g*'s in the words below.

1. charge 2. strange 3. challenge 4. engage

Part C. Study the words below and answer the questions which follow.

1. change + ing = changing change + able = changeable
2. outrage + ed = outraged outrage + ous = outrageous

When *-ed* and *-ing* are added to *change* and *outrage*, the final *e* is dropped.

When *-able* and *-ous* are added to *change* and *outrage*, the final *e* is kept.

What sound would the *g* have in *changeable* and *outrageous* if the silent *e* were dropped?

hard g

Pattern: When an ending that begins with *a* or *o* is added to a word that ends in *ce* or *ge*, the silent *e* is kept to retain the soft *c* and *g* sounds.

❻ Adding Endings to Words That End in *ge*. Add the endings to the words below. Remember to keep the silent *e* when necessary.

1. hinge + ing	hinging	6. challenge + ing	challenging
2. plunge + ers	plungers	7. strange + er	stranger
3. orange + ade	orangeade	8. advantage + ous	advantageous
4. revenge + ful	revengeful	9. outrage + ous + ly	outrageously
5. exchange + ing	exchanging	10. courage + ous + ly	courageously

64 Lesson 12

❺ Silent *e* Pattern 2

In this exercise, the pattern introduced in Lesson 11 is expanded to include words that end in *ge* and endings that start with *o*.

Remind students that *g* is pronounced both /g/ and /j/. The soft *g*, however, does not follow as regular a pattern as the soft *c* does. The *ge* and *gi* spellings produce both hard and soft *g*'s (*get* and *gem*, *girl* and *ginger*). But when words end in *ge*, the final sound is usually /j/.

In Part A of this exercise, students see that when *a* or *o* follows a *g*, the *g* has the hard /g/ sound. In Part B, they see that *ge* at the end of a word spells /j/.

In Part C, students discover that the silent *e* is retained when an ending that starts with *a* or *o* is added to a word that ends in *ge* in order to retain the soft *g*. If students have trouble answering the question at the end, pronounce *changable* and *outragous* using a hard *g*.

Notice that the final statement of the pattern includes words that end in *ce* as well.

❻ Adding Endings to Words That End in *ge*

As students work on this exercise, encourage them to look at their answers to the questions in Exercise 5, if necessary.

For number 4, remind students that the silent *e* is always kept when the ending begins with a consonant, as in Silent *e* Pattern 1.

Additional Activity:

When students have completed the exercise, quiz them with their books closed using the words they just built in this exercise.

7 **Puzzle.** Use the clues at the left to fill in the blocks of the puzzle. All of the answers are representative words in this lesson. When all the correct answers are filled in, the shaded blocks will spell a new word that ends in *nge*.

Clues

Clue	Answer
1. to shrink or cower in fear	C R **I** N G E
2. a limb of a tree	B R A **N** C H
3. not anything	N O **T** H I N G
4. language spoken in France	F R **E** N C H
5. what is worn on a finger	**R** I N G
6. twelfth part of a foot	I N **C** H
7. able to be altered	C **H** A N G E A B L E
8. a warm cover in bed	B L **A** N K E T
9. chew with a crunching noise	M U **N** C H
10. not right	W R O N **G**
11. to ask for a contest or duel	C H A L L **E** N G E

The new *nge* word: INTERCHANGE

Now write a sentence using the new word.

____

8 **Writing Sentences.** On the lines below, write the sentences that you hear.

1. Mr. Bond lived on a ranch when he was younger.
2. Brent speaks both French and English interchangeably.
3. An exchange student from England is staying with us.
4. Frank pinched his finger when he tried to fix the hinge.
5. We lingered in the lounge longer than we had intended to.

Lesson 12 65

7 Puzzle

Have students complete the puzzle by writing each answer word in the blocks next to the clues. When students have completed the puzzle, the word *interchange* will be spelled vertically in the shaded blocks. Have students write this word on the line provided and use it in a sentence of their own. Have them look it up in their dictionaries if they are not sure what it means.

8 Writing Sentences

Instruct students to write the sentences that you dictate, which are on the replica of the student page.

These sentences give students an opportunity to write the sight words and some of the representative words in context. Note any specific errors that students make, and design additional words, sentences, or phrases for specific problems.

In addition to the blends covered in this lesson, the patterns found in these sentences include:
—Silent *e* Pattern 1 (1)
—Silent *e* Pattern 2 (2)
—changing *y* to *i* (4)

Review of Unit 4

Blends with *n* That End Syllables

Objectives

- **Word Building:** Add ending blends to word parts to form words. Write the missing syllables of dictated words.
- **Alternative Spellings:** Review alternative spellings for /ns/ by writing dictated phrases.
- **Endings:** Add designated endings to words following Silent *e* Patterns 1 and 2.
- **Writing by Syllables:** Write dictated words one syllable at a time.
- **Composing a Sentence:** Write an original sentence using a selected word.
- **Writing Sentences:** Practice writing representative and sight words in context.
- **Composing a Paragraph:** Write an original paragraph using representative and sight words.
- **Puzzle:** Review representative and sight words by completing a crossword puzzle.

❶ Word Building

Have students add one of the ending blends to each word part to make a word. Encourage them to use all of the ending blends at least once. The answers given on the replica of the student page are examples. Many other combinations are possible. Accept all correctly spelled words.

Additional Activity:

Have students build as many words as they can think of using the blends and the word parts in different combinations. For instance, they might form *band*, *bang*, and *bank* for number 1.

Review of Unit 4

Blends with *n* That End Syllables

❶ **Word Building.** Write one of the ending blends below in each blank to make a word.

nd *nt* *nce* *nse* *nch* *nge* *ng* *nk*

1. ba nd	7. fli ng	13. ru ng
2. bu nch	8. hi nge	14. se nse
3. cha nce	9. le nd	15. shri nk
4. cru nch	10. li nt	16. sti ng
5. de nse	11. pla nt	17. stra nge
6. dra nk	12. pri nce	18. wi nce

❷ **Word Building.** Write the missing syllable of each word you hear.

1. pay ment	4. blan ket	7. of fense
2. pre tend	5. con vince	8. loung ing
3. pro nounce	6. com plaint	9. res i dence

❸ **Alternative Spellings for /ns/.** Write the phrases that you hear.

1. one ounce	6. making a difference
2. two cents	7. fence the yard
3. no nonsense	8. the past tense
4. a strong defense	9. put up the tents
5. good insurance	10. no more arguments

66 Review of Unit 4

---

❷ Word Building

This exercise requires students to isolate and spell single syllables in words of two or more syllables. Dictate the entire word, giving students time to isolate the missing syllable and write it in the blank.

❸ Alternative Spellings for /ns/

Before beginning this exercise, review the three spellings for /ns/ that were studied in Lesson 11: *nce*, *nse* , and *nts*. Remind students that *nce* is a far more common spelling than *nse*. Then dictate the phrases found on the replica of the student page.

4 Review of Silent *e* Patterns 1 and 2. Add the endings to the words below.

1. dance + ing	dancing	11. embrace + able	embraceable
2. plunge + ers	plungers	12. notice + able	noticeable
3. peace + able	peaceable	13. change + over	changeover
4. hinge + ed	hinged	14. sense + ible	sensible
5. defense + ive	defensive	15. pronounce + able	pronounceable
6. slice + ing	slicing	16. advantage + ous	advantageous
7. service + ing	servicing	17. challenge + er	challenger
8. service + able	serviceable	18. exchange + ing	exchanging
9. bruise + ed	bruised	19. courage + ous	courageous
10. revenge + ful	revengeful	20. dis + courage + ing	discouraging

5 Writing Words by Syllables. Write each word your teacher dictates by syllables. Then write the whole word on the line provided.

	First Syllable	Second Syllable	Third Syllable	Fourth Syllable	Whole Word
1.	an	nounce	ment		announcement
2.	sus	pen	sion		suspension
3.	in	fringe	ment		infringement
4.	un	re	spon	sive	unresponsive
5.	con	den	sa	tion	condensation
6.	in	vin	ci	ble	invincible

Use one of these words in a sentence.

____

Review of Unit 4 67

4 Review of Silent *e* Patterns 1 and 2

Before students begin this exercise, remind them that when a word ends in *ce* or *ge*, the silent *e* is retained if the ending begins with *a*, *o*, or a consonant.

5 Writing Words by Syllables

Dictate each word by syllables, emphasizing the syllables. Then pronounce the whole word normally. Remind students that the number of blanks indicates the number of syllables in the word.

If students have difficulty spelling the *ci* syllable in *invincible*, remind them of the soft *c* pattern.

Don't worry about formal syllable divisions. It is more important for students to spell the word correctly than to have their syllabication match that of the dictionary. In some of these words, the blends they have been learning are divided between syllables. If students write *su spen sion* instead of *sus pen sion*, for instance, accept their response.

Additional Activities:

Have students look up the meanings of any of these words that they don't already know.

Have them use the rest of the words in original sentences.

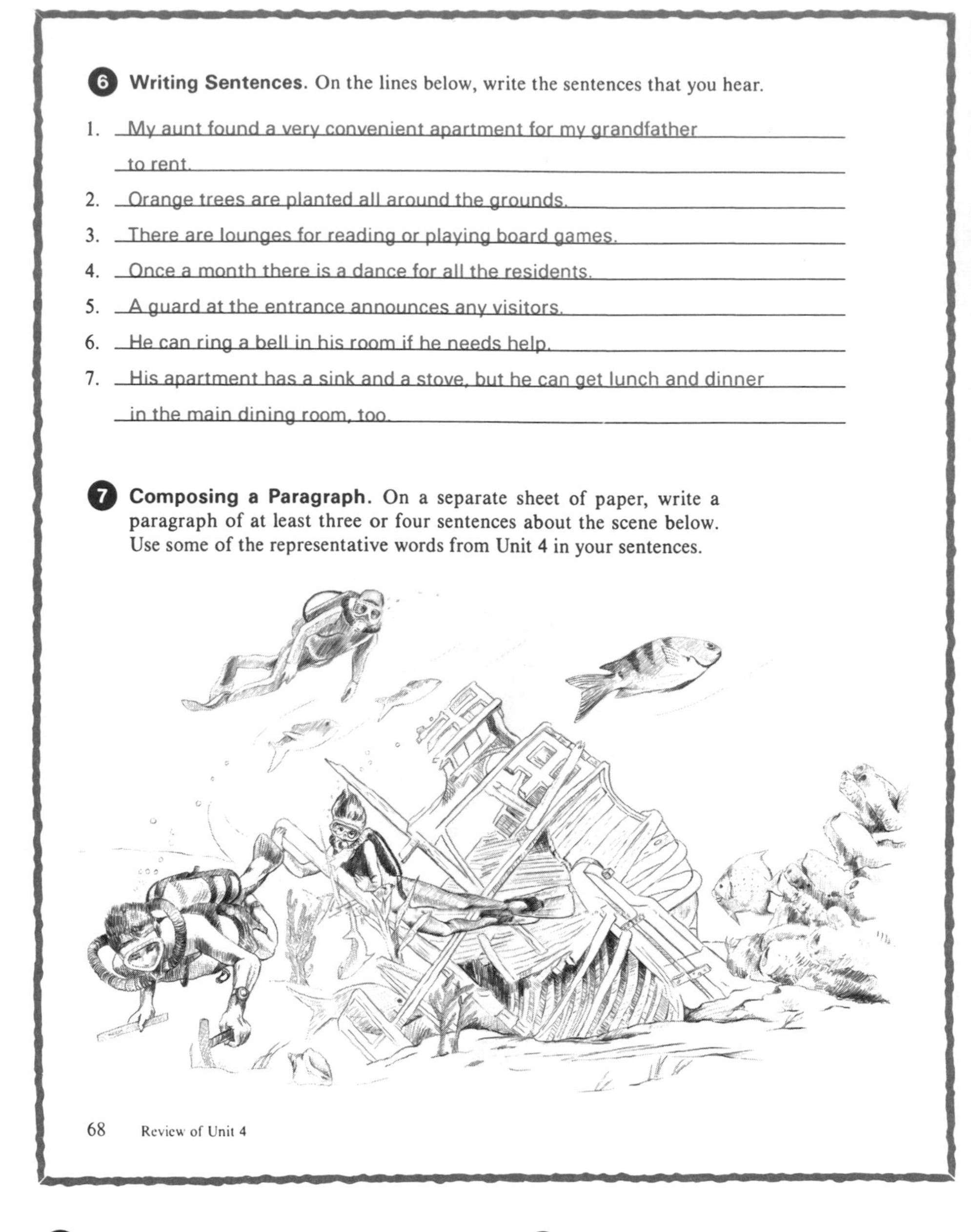
6 Writing Sentences. On the lines below, write the sentences that you hear.

1. My aunt found a very convenient apartment for my grandfather to rent.
2. Orange trees are planted all around the grounds.
3. There are lounges for reading or playing board games.
4. Once a month there is a dance for all the residents.
5. A guard at the entrance announces any visitors.
6. He can ring a bell in his room if he needs help.
7. His apartment has a sink and a stove, but he can get lunch and dinner in the main dining room, too.

7 Composing a Paragraph. On a separate sheet of paper, write a paragraph of at least three or four sentences about the scene below. Use some of the representative words from Unit 4 in your sentences.

68 Review of Unit 4

6 Writing Sentences

Instruct students to write the sentences that you dictate, which are on the replica of the student page.

These sentences give students an opportunity to write some of the representative words and sight words from this unit in context. Note any specific errors that students make, and design additional words, sentences, or phrases for specific problems.

In addition to the blends covered in this unit, the patterns found in these sentences include:
—possessive pronouns (1, 6, and 7)
—Silent *e* Pattern 1 (7)

7 Composing a Paragraph

Discuss the illustration with students before they begin to write. Encourage them to use as many representative and sight words from this unit as they can.

Encourage students to look up words they aren't sure of after they finish writing. Remember that errors in words that haven't been studied yet shouldn't be treated negatively. Point out any parts of the word that are spelled correctly and praise the effort.

8 **Crossword Puzzle.** Use the clues below to complete this crossword puzzle. Most of the answers are representative words or sight words from Unit 4 or contain the Unit 4 blends.

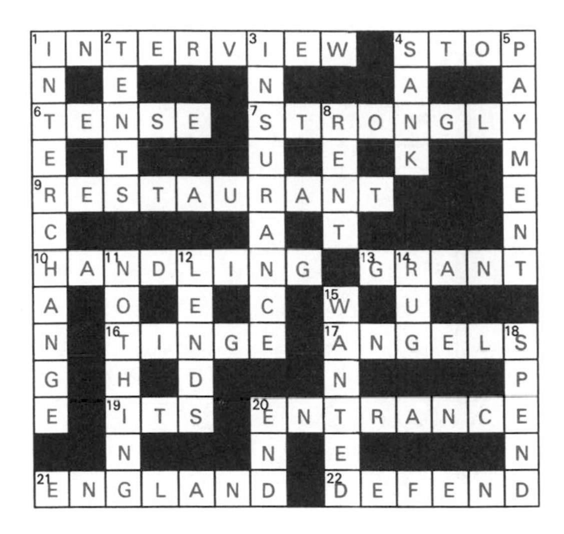

Across

1. A meeting between two people: a job ___
4. The opposite of go
6. Not relaxed
7. Powerfully or forcefully
9. A place to eat
10. Touching with the hands
13. To give or bestow: to ___ a wish
16. A trace of color
17. Heavenly beings
19. A possessive pronoun
20. An opening or doorway
21. London is its capital.
22. To protect against invaders

Down

1. To substitute for something else
2. Canvas houses
3. Protection against loss or injury
4. Fell to the bottom of the ocean
5. A sum of money paid
8. Monthly payment for an apartment
11. Not anything
12. Lets someone borrow
14. A carpet
15. Desired
18. The opposite of save
20. The opposite of beginning

Review of Unit 4 69

8 Crossword Puzzle

Have students complete the crossword puzzle. Tell them that most of the answer words are representative or sight words from Unit 4. The clues are mostly definitions that rely on the students' general knowledge.

Allow them to use a dictionary if they want to. You might want them to work in pairs or small groups. If necessary, give them the following list of answer words and have them check off words as they use them.

angels
defend
end
England
entrance
grant
handling
insurance
interchange
interview
its
lends
nothing
payment
rent
restaurant
rug
sank
spend
stop
strongly
tense
tents
tinge
wanted

Unit 4 Tests

We recommend that you test your students on the representative words and sight words from Unit 4 before going on. The following are suggested lists of representative words and sight words from Unit 4. You may want to substitute other words to meet the needs of your students.

Dictate each word and use it in a simple sentence. Students should be able to spell 90 percent of the representative words and 10 of the 12 sight words correctly.

Representative Words	Sight Words
1. respond	1. view
2. chance	2. finger
3. infant	3. England
4. sentence	4. longer
5. payments	5. restaurant
6. standing	6. guard
7. sense	7. linger
8. lunch	8. interview
9. inch	9. younger
10. hinge	10. review
11. important	11. English
12. license	12. guardian
13. longing	
14. exchange	
15. cringe	
16. expense	
17. banking	
18. thankful	
19. handful	
20. difference	

Lesson 13

The Blends *mp*, *sp*, *st*, and *sk*

Objectives

- **Blends:** Learn to spell words with the ending blends *mp*, *sp*, *st*, and *sk*
- **Sight Words:** Learn to spell *hoist*, *moist*, *personal*, *personnel*, *work*, and *clerk*. Learn to discriminate between *personal* and *personnel*.
- **Composing Sentences:** Write original sentences using designated and selected words.
- **Sound Discrimination:** Discriminate between words that end in *sk* and *st*.
- **Compound Words:** Form compound words with both elements given.
- **Suffixes:** Discover the use of the comparative and superlative suffixes *-er* and *-est*. Add *-er* and *-est* to designated words. Write dictated phrases containing *-er* and *-est*.
- **Pattern:** Discover when to use the suffixes *-er* and *-est* and when to use *more* and *most* to show comparisons.
- **Writing Sentences:** Practice writing representative and sight words in context.

Sight Words

Teach the sight words using the methods described on pages 9-12 in the introduction to this book.

Point out the *oi* spelling in *hoist* and *moist*. This spelling will be covered in detail in Book 4 of this series. Note that both *personal* and *personnel* are built from the word *person*.

Point out that *work* and *clerk* rhyme, even though *work* is spelled with *o* and *clerk* is spelled with *e*. These are *r*-controlled vowels and will be dealt with in Lessons 17 and 18 of this book as well as in Book 4.

Lesson 13

The Blends *mp*, *sp*, *st*, and *sk*

Sight Words		
hoist	personal	work
moist	personnel	clerk

Blends
mp
sp
st
sk

1 Listening

Listen to the sound of *mp* in these words.

damp	empty	bump	company
camping	impish	pumpkin	slumping

Listen to the sound of *sp* in these words.

lisp	gasp	clasp
crisp	wasp	grasp

Listen to the sound of *st* in these words.

fast	cost	first	mostly
past	crust	assist	dentist

Listen to the sound of *sk* in these words.

ask	desk	dusk	brisk
mask	disk	basketball	risking

2 Writing Words. On the lines below, write the words that you hear.

1. crisp	4. empty	7. dentist
2. first	5. task	8. company
3. risky	6. grasping	9. costly

70 Lesson 13

1 Listening

Introduce the words with the blend *mp* using the following steps.

1. Say the sound /mp/ and ask students what letters make the sound.
2. Say the letters *m-p* and ask students what sound they make.
3. Say the word *damp* and ask students what letters spell /da/ and what letters spell /mp/.
4. Say the word *damp* and ask students what letters spell *damp*.

Follow the same steps to introduce the words with the blends *sp*, *st*, and *sk*. Contrast the different sounds for *a* in *gasp* and *wasp*.

Make sure that students know the meanings of all the representative words before going on with the lesson.

2 Writing Words

Instruct students to write the words that you dictate, which are found on the replica of the student page. Say each word, use it in a phrase or sentence, and say the word again.

3 Sight Words: *Personal* and *Personnel*. The words *personal* and *personnel* are often confused. Look up both words in your dictionary and write a definition for each word below.

personal having to do with a particular person; private; one's own

personnel the people employed by a business or organization

Use each word in a sentence of your own.

personal ______

personnel ______

4 Distinguishing Between *sk* and *st*. Underline the word that you hear in each pair below.

1. mask — mast
2. dusk — dust
3. whisk — whist
4. musk — must
5. cask — cast
6. risk — wrist

5 Word Building: Compound Words. Build the compound words below. All of these words are closed compounds.

1. task + master taskmaster
2. camp + ground campground
3. clock + work clockwork
4. break + fast breakfast
5. color + fast colorfast
6. sales + clerk salesclerk
7. out + cast outcast
8. hand + clasp handclasp
9. team + work teamwork
10. fore + most foremost

Use three of these words in sentences. Look up the words in a dictionary if necessary.

1. ______
2. ______
3. ______

Lesson 13 71

3 Sight Words: *Personal* and *Personnel*

Many people confuse *personal* and *personnel*, even though they are not homonyms. This exercise provides an opportunity for students to learn the differences in their meanings and to use each of them in original sentences. Encourage students to put the definitions into their own words.

4 Distinguishing Between *sk* and *st*

Some students have difficulty discriminating between the *sk* and *st* blends. This exercise is designed to help you identify students with this difficulty.

Dictate the following list of words, instructing students to underline the one they hear in each pair found on the student page.

1. mask
2. dust
3. whisk
4. must
5. cast
6. risk

If students have difficulty with this exercise, spend some time with them individually, helping them to hear the differences in these sounds. Dictate the words and ask students to write them. Ask students to read the list of words to you, listening carefully to their pronunciation. Model the correct sounds for them. Make up other syllable and word pairs for continued practice, if necessary.

5 Word Building: Compound Words

In this exercise, students combine two words to form a new compound word. Be sure they know the meanings of all the compound words before they write their sentences.

Additional Activity:

Have students write as many compound words as they can using *first* as one element. Have them check their dictionaries to see whether their compounds are closed, hyphenated, or open.

6 The Suffixes *-er* and *-est*. The suffixes *-er* and *-est* are added to adjectives and adverbs to show comparisons.

Part A: Study these examples and fill in the blanks in the pattern which follows.

-er	*-est*
1. This desk is *bigger* than that one.	This is the *biggest* house on the block.
2. We're *closer* to home than we were.	Tonight he came the *closest* to winning.
3. Your mask is *scarier* than mine.	She wore the *scariest* mask I've ever seen.

Pattern: When two things are being compared, add the suffix -er.

When three or more things are being compared, add the suffix -est.

Part B: Add the suffixes to the words below. Follow the patterns that you have studied for adding endings.

1. slim + er	slimmer	6. crunchy + est	crunchiest
2. bumpy + est	bumpiest	7. flat + er	flatter
3. brave + est	bravest	8. pretty + er	prettier
4. costly + er	costlier	9. strange + est	strangest
5. blue + er	bluer	10. crusty + er	crustier

Part C: On the lines below, write the phrases that you hear. Remember to follow the patterns that you have learned for adding endings.

1. the dampest basement	6. the greener grass
2. the dimmer light	7. Tuesday's earliest train
3. the latest news	8. the drier crust
4. the thinner blanket	9. the youngest camper
5. the gravest danger	10. the fastest runner

72 Lesson 13

6 The Suffixes *-er* and *-est*

This exercise draws students' attention to the way the comparative and superlative forms of adjectives and adverbs are formed and used.

In Part A the two suffixes are modeled, and students discover the pattern by filling in the blanks. In Part B students add *-er* and *-est* to given words, and in Part C they write some of these forms from dictation. When doing Parts B and C, remind students to follow the patterns for adding endings that they have studied.

If students have trouble with number 5, *bluer*, point out that this word ends in a silent *e*, which is dropped. Most of the practice students have had with Silent *e* Pattern 1 has been with **V**Ce words.

For Part C, dictate the phrases found on the replica of the student page, allowing enough time for students to analyze the words if necessary.

Additional Activity:

Have students identify the patterns followed when they added the endings to the words in Part B.

7 More about Comparisons

Part A: Write the root word for each of the words below and answer the question that follows.

1. damper	damp	5. shadiest	shady
2. fastest	fast	6. brighter	bright
3. emptier	empty	7. crisper	crisp
4. craziest	crazy	8. thirstier	thirst *or* thirsty

How many syllables do the root words have? one or two

Part B: Study the examples below and answer the question.

Comparing two things: 1. This sunset is *more beautiful* than the one last night.
2. Is this game *more important* than next week's game?

Comparing three or more things: 1. These are the *most beautiful* flowers in the garden.
2. This is the *most important* interview I've had.

How many syllables do *beautiful* and *important* have? three

Now fill in the blanks in the pattern below.

Pattern: The suffixes er and est are usually added to words with one or two syllables to show comparison.
The words more and most are usually used with words of three or more syllables to show comparison.

8 Writing Sentences.

On the lines below, write the sentences that you hear.

1. My dentist is a personal friend of mine.
2. In this damp weather, everything feels moist.
3. That company is going to hire someone to work the hoist.
4. The personnel assistant is hiring three new salesclerks.
5. Their basketball team plays a brisker game than ours does.

Lesson 13 73

7 More about Comparisons

This exercise draws attention to the fact that *-er* and *-est* are usually added to words of one or two syllables, and that *more* and *most* are used with longer words to show comparison. Remind students that we never use both *-er* and *more* or *-est* and *most* together. In other words, we don't write "more faster" or "most fastest."

In part A, accept either *thirsty* or *thirst* as the root word for number 8.

8 Writing Sentences

Instruct students to write the sentences that you dictate, which are on the replica of the student page.

These sentences give students an opportunity to write the sight words and some of the representative words in context. Note any specific errors that students make, and design additional words, sentences, or phrases for specific problems.

In addition to the blends covered in this lesson, the patterns found in these sentences include:
—possessive pronouns (1 and 5)
—compound words (2, 3, 4, and 5)
—Silent *e* Pattern 1 (4)
—comparatives (5)

Lesson 14

The Blends *lt*, *ld*, and *lm*

Objectives

- **Blends:** Learn to spell words with the ending blends *lt*, *ld*, and *lm*.
- **Sight Words:** Learn to spell *world*, *soldier*, *captain*, *sergeant*, *worth*, and *forth*. Use the sight words to complete sentences.
- **Word Building:** Add ending blends to word parts to form words.
- **Homonyms:** Distinguish between homonyms that end in /ld/.
- **Apostrophes:** Review various uses of the apostrophe by writing dictated phrases and sentences.
- **Compound Words:** Form compound words with both elements given.
- **Composing Sentences:** Write original sentences using selected words.
- **Writing Sentences:** Practice writing the representative and sight words in context.
- **Puzzle:** Use representative and sight words to complete a puzzle.

Lesson 14

The Blends *lt*, *ld*, and *lm*

Sight Words		
world	captain	worth
soldier	sergeant	forth

Blends: *lt*, *ld*, *lm*

1 Listening

Listen to the sound of *lt* in these words.

belt	wilt	colt	result
felt	built	adult	consult
melting	quilt	saltiest	difficult

Listen to the sound of *ld* in these words.

bold	child	field
behold	rebuild	golden
foretold	building	shoulder

Listen to the sound of *lm* in these words.

elm	helm	realm
film	helmet	overwhelm

2 Writing Words. On the lines below, write the words that you hear.

1. adult
2. filmed
3. children
4. helmet
5. shoulder
6. built
7. overwhelm
8. revolt
9. withholding

74 Lesson 14

Sight Words

Teach the sight words using the methods described on pages 9-12 in the introduction to this book.

Contrast the pronunciation of *or* in *world* and *worth* with that in *forth*. Point out that *forth* is a homonym of the ordinal number *fourth*. Note the /ar/ pronunciation of *er* in *sergeant*. Point out also that the second *e* in *sergeant* gives the *g* a soft sound.

1 Listening

Introduce the words with the blend *lt* using the following steps.

1. Say the sound /lt/ and ask students what letters make the sound.
2. Say the letters *l-t* and ask students what sound they make.
3. Say the word *belt* and ask students what letters spell /be/ and what letters spell /lt/.
4. Say the word *belt* and ask students what letters spell *belt*.

Follow the same steps to introduce the words with the blends *ld* and *lm*.

Point out the *ui* spellings in *built*, *rebuild*, and *building*. Note that these words are all related to *build*, a sight word in Lesson 2. Point out the *ou* in *shoulder* and the *a* in *realm*. If students have a great deal of trouble learning to spell any of these words, suggest that they make a mental picture of the spelling of the word.

Make sure that students know the meanings of all the representative words before going on with the lesson.

2 Writing Words

Instruct students to write the words that you dictate, which are found on the replica of the student page. Say each word, use it in a phrase or simple sentence, and say the word again.

3 Using Sight Words. Fill in each blank in the sentences below with one of the sight words from this lesson. Use each word only once.

1. A person in the army is called a soldier.
2. A captain has a higher rank than a sergeant.
3. A sergeant has a higher rank than a private.
4. Frank bought three dollars' worth of gasoline.
5. The Chases took a cruise around the world.
6. Who was the first to come forth when the captain asked for volunteers?

4 Word Building. Write one of the blends from this lesson in each of the blanks below to form a word. Do not make the same word twice.

1. bo ld
2. bo lt
3. co ld
4. co lt
5. e lm
6. fi lm
7. gui lt
8. ha lt
9. he lm
10. jo lt
11. mi ld
12. mo ld
13. sco ld
14. ti lt
15. yie ld

5 Homonyms That End in /ld/. Words that end in *ld* often sound like the past tense of words that end with *l*. Choose the correct word in each of the sentences below and write it on the line provided. Use your dictionary if you need to.

1. Glenn (bold/bowled) very well last night. bowled
2. A (bald/balled) eagle has white feathers on its head. bald
3. Hope (weld/welled) up in Grace's heart. welled
4. I (told/tolled) Kent to go home. told
5. Pris's boots needed to be (resold/resoled). resoled
6. Who (build/billed) you for the repairs? billed

Lesson 14 75

3 Using Sight Words

This exercise gives students additional practice in writing the sight words from this lesson by using them to complete sentences.

4 Word Building

Have students add one of the ending blends in this lesson to each word part to make a word. The answers given on the replica of the student page are examples. Accept all correctly spelled words.

5 Homonyms That End in /ld/

This exercise requires the student to distinguish verbs ending with *led* or *lled* from a variety of words ending with *ld*. Remind students that the spelling of a homonym is determined by its meaning in the context of the sentence.

6 Reviewing the Apostrophe. Write the phrases and sentences that you hear. Use an apostrophe when necessary.

1. Steve can't go.
2. Shirley's child
3. my two aunts' quilts
4. I've got a cold.
5. twenty members' votes
6. the V.I.P.'s lounge
7. It's bound to happen.
8. They're first on the list.
9. many soldiers' uniforms
10. That's Frank's belt.

7 Word Building: Compound Words. Build the compound words below. All of these are closed compounds.

1. with + hold ___withhold___
2. film + goer ___filmgoer___
3. up + hold ___uphold___
4. salt + box ___saltbox___
5. helms + man ___helmsman___
6. film + strip ___filmstrip___
7. ten + fold ___tenfold___
8. thunder + bolt ___thunderbolt___
9. worth + while ___worthwhile___
10. house + hold ___household___

Use two of these compound words in sentences.

1. ______
2. ______

8 Writing Sentences. On the lines below, write the sentences that you hear.

1. The sergeant tightened the strap on his helmet.
2. Harold saw a lot of the world when he was a soldier.
3. The captain told his men the results of the field test.
4. You're the fourth adult to come forth and offer to help.
5. Do you know what the school's building fund is worth now?

76 Lesson 14

6 Reviewing the Apostrophe

Dictate the phrases and sentences found on the replica of the student page. If you have students who are having difficulty with the possessive apostrophe, review the steps introduced in Lesson 1 before beginning this exercise.

The primary purpose of this exercise is to review the various uses of the apostrophe that students have studied. However, this exercise also provides an opportunity to review when to use a capital letter at the beginning of a sentence and a period at the end. Numbers 1, 4, 7, 8, and 10 are short sentences and should begin with capital letters and end with periods. Numbers 2, 3, 5, 6, and 9 are phrases and should not have periods at the end. Number 2 begins with a capitalized proper name, but the other phrases should not begin with capitals.

If students have not mastered the possessive apostrophe, design additional exercises for them, guiding them through the procedure until it becomes automatic.

Give them phrases such as "the soldier's helmet." Have them say the owner (soldier) without adding what is owned. Then they should write down *soldier*. Next they should write an apostrophe. Finally they should add an *s*, since they can hear one when they say the phrase. Follow the same procedure with plural nouns ending in *s*.

7 Word Building: Compound Words

Have students look up the meanings of any of these compound words they don't already know before using two of them in sentences.

8 Writing Sentences

Instruct students to write the sentences that you dictate, which are on the replica of the student page.

These sentences give students an opportunity to write the sight words and some of the representative words in context. Note any specific errors that students make, and design additional words, sentences, or phrases for specific problems.

In addition to the blends covered in this lesson, the patterns found in these sentences include:

—possessive pronouns (1 and 3)
—contractions (4)
—homonyms (4)
—possessives (5)

9 Puzzle. Use the clues below to fill in the blocks of the puzzle. Refer to the list of answer words at the bottom of the page if you need to. When you have filled in all the correct answers, the letters in the shaded blocks will spell a military rank between sergeant and captain.

Clues

Clue	Answer
1. A structure for living or working in	B U I **L** D I N G
2. A person who serves in an army	S O L D **I** E R
3. Changing from solid to liquid by heating	M **E** L T I N G
4. Where the arm attaches to the body	S H O **U** L D E R
5. Units used to measure electricity	V O L **T** S
6. People who live under the same roof	H O U S **E** H O L D
7. The color of a metal used for jewelry	G O L D E **N**
8. Grown up	**A** D U L T
9. Making a motion picure	F I L M I **N** G
10. An officer in the army	C A P **T** A I N

The military rank: LIEUTENANT

Word List

adult
building
captain
filming
golden
household
melting
shoulder
soldier
volts

Lesson 14 77

9 Puzzle

Have students complete the puzzle by writing each answer word in the boxes next to the clue. An alphabetized list of answers is provided at the bottom of the page.

When students have completed the puzzle, the word *lieutenant* will be spelled vertically in the shaded boxes. Have students write this word on the line provided.

Additional Activity:

Students may enjoy developing this type of puzzle themselves. Have them work in small groups and use the word lists at the back of the book. They should begin by selecting a word to be spelled out vertically. Then words that contain the letters of the vertical word are selected and defined. The grid is arranged so that the letters that spell the vertical word are lined up with each other.

When the groups have finished designing their puzzles, have them exchange puzzles and solve them.

Lesson 15

The Blends *lk*, *lp*, and *lf*

Objectives

- **Blends:** Learn to spell words with the ending blends *lk*, *lp*, and *lf*.
- **Sight Words:** Learn to spell *folk*, *yolk*, *look*, *listen*, *down*, and *bought*. Use the sight words to complete sentences.
- **Endings:** Add *-s* or *-es* to words that end in *lf*.
- **Compound Words:** Form compound words that begin with *self*. Learn that these words are hyphenated.
- **Composing Sentences:** Write original sentences using designated reflexive pronouns and selected words.
- **Writing by Syllables:** Write dictated words one syllable at a time.
- **Root Words:** Identify the root words of designated words.
- **Comparisons:** Review comparative and superlative forms.
- **Writing Sentences:** Practice writing representative and sight words in context.

Sight Words

Teach the sight words using the methods described on pages 9-12 in the introduction to this book.

Point out the silent *l* in *folk* and *yolk*, and contrast these words with the representative words that contain the blend *lk*. Note also the silent *t* in *listen*, and the *ough* spelling in *bought*. Strategies for remembering silent letters are presented in Unit 6 of this book.

Lesson 15

The Blends *lk*, *lp*, and *lf*

Sight Words		
folk	look	down
yolk	listen	bought

Blends

1 Listening

lk — Listen to the sound of *lk* in these words.

elk	hulk	silk
bulk	sulking	buttermilk

lp — Listen to the sound of *lp* in these words.

help	gulps	pulp
helper	scalp	pulpiness

lf — Listen to the sound of *lf* in these words.

shelf	wolf	gulf
selfish	golfing	engulf

2 Writing Words. On the lines below, write the words that you hear.

1. shelf	4. milkman	7. golfer
2. silk	5. myself	8. pulpy
3. scalp	6. bulky	9. helpless

78 Lesson 15

1 Listening

Introduce the words with the blend *lk* using the following steps.

1. Say the sound /lk/ and ask students what letters make the sound.
2. Say the letters *l-k* and ask students what sound they make.
3. Say the word *elk* and ask students what letter spells /ĕ/, and what letters spell /lk/.
4. Say the word *elk* and ask students what letters spell *elk*.

Follow the same steps to introduce the words with the blends *lp* and *lf*.

Make sure that students know the meanings of all the representative words before going on with the lesson.

2 Writing Words

Instruct students to write the words that you dictate, which are found on the replica of the student page. Say each word, use it in a phrase or simple sentence, and say the word again.

3 Using Sight Words. Use one of the sight words from this lesson to complete each sentence.

1. Gramps ___bought___ a new suit to wear to the wedding.
2. A chicken egg is made up of the white and the ___yolk___.
3. Did the boss ___look___ at Phyllis's progress report?
4. I love to ___listen___ to the talk shows on the radio.
5. Ralph played the guitar and sang ___folk___ songs at the party.
6. All the decorations had to be taken ___down___ after the holidays.

4 Adding *-s* or *-es* to Words That End in *lf*. Some words that end in *lf* change the *f* to *v* before *-es* is added. For verbs that end in *lf* and for a few nouns also, the *f* is kept and *-s* is added. Add *-s* or *-es* to the words below. Use your dictionary when necessary.

1. self	selves	5. shelf	shelves
2. half	halves	6. wolf	wolves (n.)
3. elf	elves	7. gulf	gulfs
4. golf	golfs	8. engulf	engulfs

5 Using the Dictionary: Compound Words with *Self*. Make the compound words indicated. Use your dictionary to determine whether they should be closed, open, or hyphenated compounds.

1. self + conscious	self-conscious	5. self + made	self-made
2. self + supporting	self-supporting	6. self + doubt	self-doubt
3. self + pity	self-pity	7. self + control	self-control
4. self + respect	self-respect	8. self + help	self-help

All of these words have a ___hyphen___ between the two parts.

Lesson 15 79

3 Using Sight Words

This exercise gives students additional practice in writing the sight words from this lesson by using them to complete sentences.

4 Adding *-s* or *-es* to Words That End in *lf*

This exercise reviews the *f* to *v* pattern learned in Book 2 but draws students' attention to the fact that this pattern does not hold true for all words that end in *lf*. Remind students that when they pronounce these words, they can hear the ones that change from *f* to *v*.

Check to be sure students have retained the *f* and added *s* to numbers 4, 7, and 8.

You may want to point out that when *wolf* is used as a verb, the *f* is retained and *s* is added, as in the sentence "He *wolfs* down his food."

5 Using the Dictionary: Compound Words with *Self*

In this exercise, students become familiar with several compound words that are formed with *self*. They also learn that compound words that begin with *self* are generally hyphenated.

6 Creating Sentences. Write sentences using the words that are formed by adding *self* to the personal pronouns.

1. myself: __________
2. yourself: __________
3. himself: __________
4. herself: __________
5. itself: __________
6. ourselves: __________
7. yourselves: __________
8. themselves: __________

7 Writing Words by Syllables. Write each word your teacher dictates by syllables. Then write the whole word on the line provided.

	First Syllable	Second Syllable	Third Syllable	Fourth Syllable	Whole Word
1.	as	ter	isk		asterisk
2.	hos	pi	tal		hospital
3.	with	hold	ing		withholding
4.	dif	fi	cul	ty	difficulty
5.	as	pi	ra	tion	aspiration
6.	con	sul	ta	tion	consultation
7.	un	em	ploy	ment	unemployment
8.	un	self	ish	ness	unselfishness

Use two of these words in sentences.

1. __________
2. __________

80 Lesson 15

6 Creating Sentences

In this exercise, students use the personal pronouns formed with *self* in original sentences. Point out that these compound words that end in *self* are not hyphenated.

Encourage students to write freely and to look up the spelling of words they have not yet studied.

Remember that errors in words that haven't been studied yet shouldn't be treated negatively. Point out any parts of the word that are spelled correctly and praise the effort.

7 Writing Words by Syllables

Dictate the words by syllables, emphasizing the syllables and having students write them on the lines provided. Then pronounce the whole word normally. Remind students that the number of blanks indicates the number of syllables in the word.

Don't be concerned about formal syllable divisions. In some of these words, the blends students have been studying are divided between syllables. If students write *hosp i tal* instead of *hos pi tal*, for instance, accept their response. It is more important for them to spell the word correctly than to have their syllabication match that of the dictionary.

Additional Activities:

Have students look up the meanings of any of these words that they don't already know.

Have them use the rest of the words in original sentences.

8 Finding Root Words. Write the root word for each of the words below.

1. silkiest	silk	7. shelving	shelf
2. unclasped	clasp	8. unmasked	mask
3. behalf	half	9. bulkiness	bulk
4. assistance	assist	10. resulting	result
5. diskette	disk	11. unhelpful	help
6. milkiness	milk	12. rebuilding	build

9 Review of Comparisons. Fill in the blank in each sentence below with the correct form of the word in parentheses.

1. (risky)	Jack's stunt is riskier than Fred's.
2. (hot)	Today is the hottest day we've had all summer.
3. (funny)	Chris's joke was funnier than the one Grant told.
4. (spectacular)	That was the most spectacular stunt I've ever seen.
5. (safe)	They tried to make the race course safer than it was.
6. (suspicious)	That letter was the most suspicious clue the detective found.

10 Writing Sentences. On the lines below, write the sentences that you hear.

1. Donald can't eat egg yolks or salty foods.
2. We saw the hulk of an old battleship out in the gulf.
3. We sat down by ourselves and listened to folk songs.
4. The dictionary I bought yesterday will be more helpful than the old one.
5. If you would only look at yourselves, you'd see how selfish you are being.

Lesson 15 81

8 Finding Root Words

In this exercise, students can see the relationship between a word and the root word from which it was built. Be sure students remove both the prefix and the suffix from words in numbers 2, 8, 11, and 12. You may decide to allow *silky*, *milky*, and *bulky* for numbers 1, 6, and 9. If you do, discuss the fact that each of these words also contains a root word.

9 Review of Comparisons

This exercise reviews comparative and superlative forms of adjectives. Remind students to follow the patterns that they have studied for adding endings. If necessary, review when to use *-er* and *-est* and when to use *more* and *most* before students begin.

10 Writing Sentences

Instruct students to write the sentences that you dictate, which are on the replica of the student page.

These sentences give students an opportunity to write the sight words and some of the representative words in context. Note any specific errors that students make, and design additional words, sentences, or phrases for specific problems.

In addition to the blends covered in this lesson, the patterns found in these sentences include:
—contractions (1 and 5)
—compound words (2, 3, and 5)
—personal pronouns with *self* (3 and 5)
—comparatives (4)

Lesson 16

The Blends *ct*, *ft*, *pt*, and *xt*

Objectives

- **Blends:** Learn to spell words with the ending blends *ct*, *ft*, *pt*, and *xt*.
- **Sight Words:** Learn to spell *indict*, *example*, *sample*, *simple*, *ghost*, and *ghetto*.
- **Word Building:** Form nouns from verbs that end in *ct* or *pt* by adding *-ion*. Learn a strategy for predicting the spelling of /shən/.
- **Suffixes:** Add the suffixes *-ion*, *-cian*, *-sion*, and *-tion* to root words.
- **Compound Words:** Match words to form compound words.
- **Composing Sentences:** Write original sentences using selected words.
- **Alternative Spellings:** Learn that /kt/ at the end of words can be spelled *ct* or *cked*.
- **Dictionary Skills:** Use the dictionary to find the correct spelling of words that end in /kt/.
- **Writing Sentences:** Practice writing representative and sight words in context.
- **Composing a Paragraph:** Write an original paragraph using representative and sight words.

Sight Words

Teach the sight words using the methods described on pages 9-12 in the introduction to this book.

Point out the silent *c* in *indict* and the silent *h* in *ghost* and *ghetto*.

Lesson 16

The Blends *ct*, *ft*, *pt*, and *xt*

Sight Words		
indict	sample	ghost
example	simple	ghetto

Blends

1 Listening

ct — Listen to the sound of *ct* in these words.

act	affect	strict	elected
exact	object	district	direct
react	perfect	verdict	connect
attract	intellect	suspect	contract

ft — Listen to the sound of *ft* in these words.

gift	lift	raft	soft
sift	drift	draft	left
swift	thrifty	handicraft	theft

pt — Listen to the sound of *pt* in these words.

apt	kept	accept	prompt
adapt	slept	concept	abrupt
adopt	Egypt	attempt	interrupt

xt — Listen to the sound of *xt* in these words.

next	text	context

2 Writing Words. On the lines below, write the words that you hear.

1. wept	4. context	7. defect
2. next	5. Egypt	8. objection
3. connect	6. except	9. disinfect

82 Lesson 16

1 Listening

Introduce the words with the blend *ct* using the following steps.

1. Say the sound /kt/ and ask students what letters make the sound.
2. Say the letters *c-t* and ask students what sound they make.
3. Say the word *act* and ask students what letters spell /a/ and what letters spell /kt/.
4. Say the word *act* and ask students what letters spell *act*.

Follow the same steps to introduce the words with the blends *ft*, *pt*, and *xt*.

Make sure that students know the meanings of all the representative words before going on with the lesson.

2 Writing Words

Instruct students to write the words that you dictate, which are found on the replica of the student page. Say each word, use it in a phrase or simple sentence, and say the word again.

3 Word Building with the Suffix *-ion*. In Lesson 6 you learned that nouns can be formed from verbs by adding the suffix *-tion*. When the verb ends in *ct* or *pt*, the suffix *-ion* is usually added to form the noun.

Build these words and answer the question below. Use the dictionary to check your spellings.

1. adopt + ion	adoption	6. act + ion	action
2. connect + ion	connection	7. erupt + ion	eruption
3. except + ion	exception	8. restrict + ion	restriction
4. infect + ion	infection	9. elect + ion	election
5. affect + ion	affection	10. disrupt + ion	disruption

If you hear /k/ or /p/ before /shən/, how is the /shən/ spelled? tion

4 Adding Suffixes. Add one of the suffixes below to each of these words. Remember that sometimes the root word changes or other letters are added before you add the suffix. Pronounce the new word before you spell it. Use the dictionary to check your spellings.

-ion *-cian* *-sion* *-tion*

1. interrupt	interruption	11. permit	permission
2. explain	explanation	12. contract	contraction
3. react	reaction	13. concept	conception
4. confess	confession	14. electric	electrician
5. educate	education	15. perfect	perfection
6. adapt	adaptation	16. complicate	complication
7. object	objection	17. transport	transportation
8. create	creation	18. televise	television
9. expect	expectation	19. subtract	subtraction
10. beauty	beautician	20. translate	translation

Lesson 16 83

3 Word Building with the Suffix *-ion*

Before students begin this exercise, review the suffixes *-tion* and *-sion* that can be used to form nouns from verbs. Remind students that they are both pronounced /shən/, and that it is sometimes difficult to remember whether /shən/ is spelled *-tion* or *-sion*, although *-tion* is more common.

Tell students that when verbs end in *ct* or *pt*, they can usually just add *-ion* to form the noun. That is the case with all the verbs in this exercise.

When students have finished building the words, have them answer the question that follows. This pattern gives students a useful strategy for determining the spelling of /shən/ in some words, i.e., if they hear /k/ or /p/ before /shən/, the ending will be spelled *-tion.*

4 Adding Suffixes

In this exercise, students must select the correct suffix to add to each word. Remind students that when the suffixes in this exercise are added, sometimes the spelling of the root word changes or other letters are added. This is particularly true of *-tion* and *-sion* words. However, these changes can usually be heard. Therefore, students should pronounce the word with the suffix added before trying to spell it.

When you go over this exercise with students, point out that number 6, *adaptation*, and number 9, *expectation*, are exceptions to the pattern followed in Exercise 3, i.e., adding *-ion* to verbs that end in *ct* or *pt*. These two words, together with *affectation* and *temptation*, are the only common exceptions to that pattern, however.

5 Word Building: Compound Words. Match a word from Column 2 with each word in Column 1 to make a compound word. Use each word in Column 1 only once. Check your dictionary to see if the compounds are closed, hyphenated, or open.

Column 1	Column 2	Compound Words	
air	book	1. aircraft	6. makeshift
crank	craft		
drift	drift	2. crankshaft	7. snowdrift
fork	drink		
left	hand	3. driftwood	8. soft drink
make	lift		
snow	shaft	4. forklift	9. spendthrift
soft	shift		
spend	thrift	5. left-hand	10. textbook
text	wood		

Use three of the compound words in sentences.

1. ____________________

2. ____________________

3. ____________________

6 Dictionary Skills: Finding the Correct Spelling. The blend *ct* at the end of a word sounds like the past tense of words that end in *ck*. Use the dictionary to find the correct spellings of the words spelled phonetically below. When you find the spelling that matches the meaning, write the word in the appropriate column.

Phonetic Spelling	Meaning	-ct	-cked
1. /ĭn sĕkt´/	a small animal with six legs	insect	
2. /ă tăkt´/	began a battle		attacked
3. /dē´fĕkt/	a fault or flaw	defect	
4. /ĭn flĭkt´/	to strike; to impose	inflict	
5. /flĭkt/	removed with a quick motion		flicked
6. /ĭn spĕkt´/	to examine carefully	inspect	

84 Lesson 16

5 Word Building: Compound Words

In this exercise, students build compound words by matching each word in column 1 with a word from column 2. The words on the replica of the student page are examples. A few more combinations are possible. Accept all compound words that are listed in a dictionary.

You may need to remind students where to find compound words in the dictionary. They are sometimes listed as entry words but also may be listed at the end of the entry for the first word in the compound.

Also point out that a pair of words may often be used together but may not be considered a compound word. If it is listed in a dictionary, it has achieved the status of a compound word. For instance, *soft drink* is listed as an open compound, but *soft spot* is not.

6 Dictionary Skills: Finding the Correct Spelling

In this exercise, students determine the correct spelling of a sound that has alternative spellings. Remind them that the phonetic spelling represents the way the word is pronounced. Point out that if the definition is in the past tense, the word will be spelled *cked.*

Additional Activity:

Have students use these words in sentences of their own.

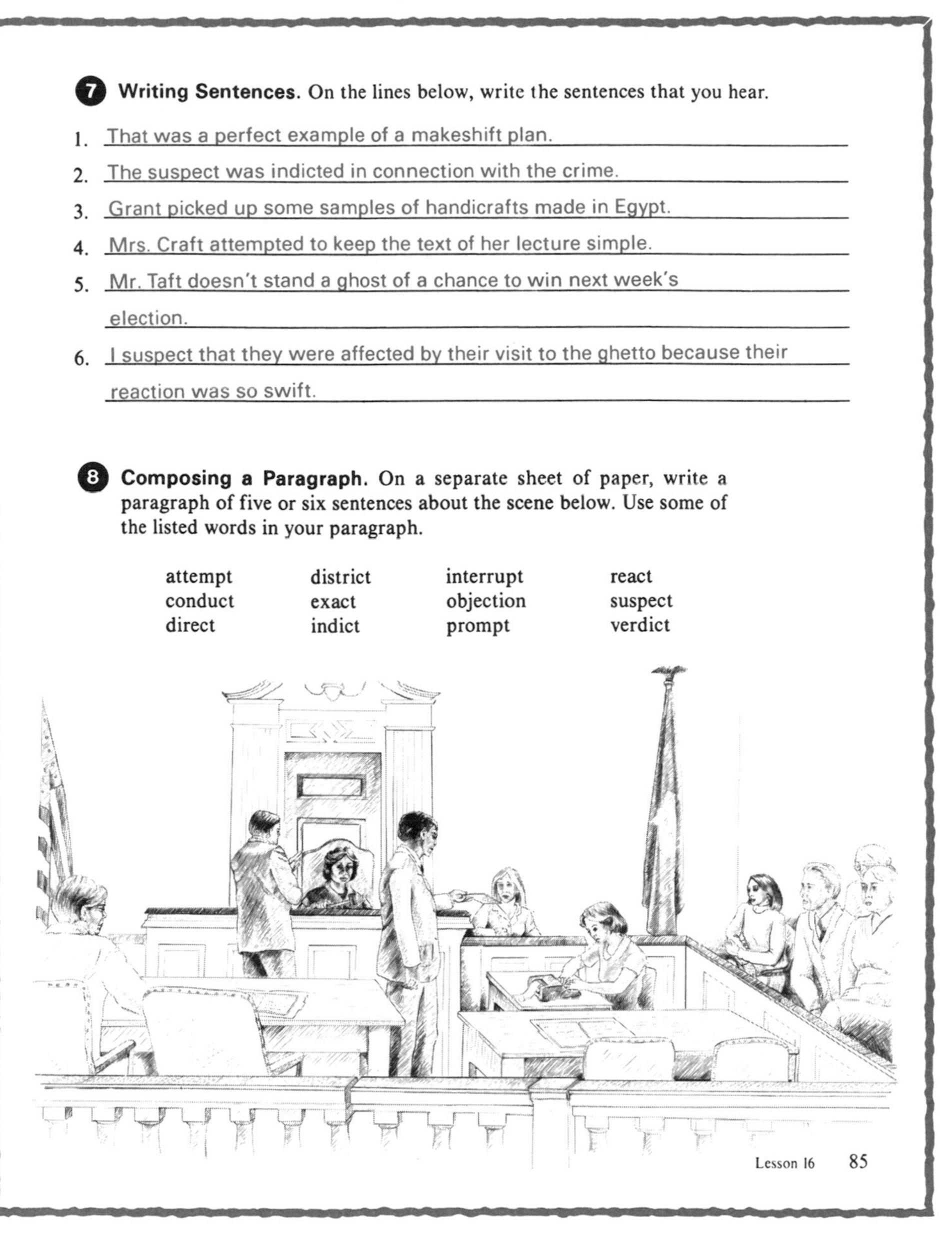

7 Writing Sentences. On the lines below, write the sentences that you hear.

1. That was a perfect example of a makeshift plan.
2. The suspect was indicted in connection with the crime.
3. Grant picked up some samples of handicrafts made in Egypt.
4. Mrs. Craft attempted to keep the text of her lecture simple.
5. Mr. Taft doesn't stand a ghost of a chance to win next week's election.
6. I suspect that they were affected by their visit to the ghetto because their reaction was so swift.

8 Composing a Paragraph. On a separate sheet of paper, write a paragraph of five or six sentences about the scene below. Use some of the listed words in your paragraph.

attempt	district	interrupt	react
conduct	exact	objection	suspect
direct	indict	prompt	verdict

Lesson 16 85

7 Writing Sentences

Instruct students to write the sentences that you dictate, which are on the replica of the student page.

These sentences give students an opportunity to write the sight words and some of the representative words in context. Note any specific errors that students make, and design additional words, sentences, or phrases for specific problems.

In addition to the blends covered in this lesson, the patterns found in these sentences include:

—compound words (1)
—words ending in /shən/ (2, 5, and 6)
—possessive pronouns (4 and 6)
—words ending in /chur/ (4)
—contractions (5)
—possessives (5)

8 Composing a Paragraph

Discuss the illustration with students before they begin to write. Encourage them to use as many of the representative words and sight words as they can.

Encourage students to look up words they aren't sure of after they finish writing. Remember that errors in words that haven't been studied yet shouldn't be treated negatively. Point out any parts of the word that are spelled correctly and praise the effort.

Lesson 17

The Blends *rd, rm, rn, rb,* and *rf*

Objectives

- **Blends:** Learn to spell words with the ending blends *rd, rm, rn, rb,* and *rf.*
- **Sight Words:** Learn to spell *bird, word, earn, learn, herb, sword, worm,* and *wharf.*
- **Word Building:** Build three words from each designated word by adding three different endings.
- **Syllable Types:** Review five types of syllables by writing examples.
- **Writing by Syllables:** Write dictated words one syllable at a time.
- **Composing Sentences:** Write original sentences using selected words.
- **Polysyllabic Words:** Use polysyllabic words to complete sentences.
- **Homonyms:** Distinguish between homonyms based on context.
- **Writing Sentences:** Practice writing representative and sight words in context.

> ## Lesson 17
>
> ### The Blends *rd, rm, rn, rb,* and *rf*
>
> | Sight Words | | | |
> |---|---|---|---|
> | bird | earn | herb | worm |
> | word | learn | sword | wharf |
>
> **Blends:** *rd*, *rm*, *rn*, *rb*, *rf*
>
> **1 Listening**
>
> Listen to the sound of *rd* in these words.
>
> | | | | |
> |---|---|---|---|
> | cord | herd | third | aboard |
> | chord | heard | regard | toward |
> | afford | hurdle | hardly | forward |
>
> Listen to the sound of *rm* in these words.
>
> | | | | |
> |---|---|---|---|
> | harm | warm | germ | storm |
> | alarm | warmth | midterm | uniform |
> | disarm | swarming | firmly | transform |
>
> Listen to the sound of *rn* in these words.
>
> | | | | |
> |---|---|---|---|
> | barn | fern | torn | turn |
> | warn | concern | tornado | burned |
> | worn | lantern | cornfield | adornment |
>
> Listen to the sound of *rb* in these words.
>
> | | | |
> |---|---|---|
> | curb | verb | superb |
> | garb | adverb | suburb |
> | garbage | proverb | disturb |
>
> Listen to the sound of *rf* in these words.
>
> | | | |
> |---|---|---|
> | surf | turf | dwarf |
> | surface | surfboard | scarf |
>
> 86 Lesson 17

Sight Words

Teach the sight words using the methods described on pages 9-12 in the introduction to this book.

These words contain the blends presented in this lesson. Since these blends all start with *r* and are ending blends, they create *r*-controlled vowels. *R*-controlled vowels will be covered in detail in Book 4 of this series. However, you should point out to students that when an *r* follows a vowel it is a signal that the spelling of the vowel may be unpredictable.

Point out the silent *h* in *herb* and the silent *w* in *sword.*

1 Listening

Since these blends all begin with *r*, it is extremely difficult to pronounce them without including a vowel sound. Furthermore, because they produce *r*-controlled vowels, it is difficult to approximate the vowel sound if it is separated from the blend. Therefore, we suggest the following variations in presenting the listening exercise in Lessons 17 and 18.

1. Use a schwa with the blends when you pronounce them by themselves.
2. Attach the vowel to the blend when you separate individual words into their phonetic parts.

Introduce the words with the blend *rd* using the following method.

T: Look at the first group of words. These words all have the blend *rd*. Listen to the sound of *rd*. (Say /ərd/.) What letters make the sound /ərd/?

S: *R-d.*

T: Good. What sound do the letters *r-d* make?

S: /ərd/.

T: Good. Listen to the sound of /ərd/ in the word *cord.* (Say *cord.*) Now listen again. (Say *cord* again.) What letter makes the sound /k/?

S: *C.*

T: Good. What letters make the /ord/ sound in *cord*?

S: *O-r-d.*

2 Writing Words. On the lines below, write the words that you hear.

1. harm	5. absorb	9. scarf
2. hard	6. garbage	10. overheard
3. warning	7. warmly	11. toward
4. surfaces	8. burned	12. concerned

3 Word Building. Add three of the endings below to each word.

able	*ed*	*ing*	*ness*
al	*er*	*less*	*y*
ance	*ful*	*ly*	

1. firm	firmer	firmly	firmness
2. harm	harmed	harmful	harmless
3. form	formal	former	formless
4. storm	storming	stormed	stormy
5. surf	surfed	surfing	surfer
6. disturb	disturbing	disturbance	disturber
7. afford	afforded	affording	affordable
8. warm	warmer	warmly	warmness
9. regard	regarded	regarding	regardless
10. hard	hardly	hardness	hardy
11. charm	charmed	charming	charmer
12. inform	informed	informer	informal
13. forward	forwarded	forwardness	forwardable
14. transform	transforming	transformable	transformer
15. perform	performed	performer	performance

Lesson 17 87

T: Good. What letters spell *cord*?
S: *C-o-r-d.*
T: Good.

Follow the same steps to introduce the words with the blends *rm*, *rn*, *rb*, and *rf*.

Draw students' attention to some of the words in which the same vowel sound is spelled differently, such as *herd/third/hurdle*, *germ/firmly*, and *curb/verb*. Also point out different pronunciations for the same spelling, such as *harm/warm*, *barn/warn*, and *dwarf/scarf*.

Make sure that students know the meanings of all the representative words before going on with the lesson.

2 Writing Words

Instruct students to write the words that you dictate, which are found on the replica of the student page. Say each word, use it in a phrase or simple sentence, and say the word again.

3 Word Building

In this exercise, students are asked to form three different words from each root using the suffixes listed. The answers on the replica of the student page are examples. Accept all correctly spelled words.

4 Review of Syllable Types. Write two other examples of each of the syllable types listed below.

Syllable Type	Example	Your Examples	
closed	curb	________	________
open	go	________	________
Cle	ble	________	________
double vowel	steel	________	________
VCe	fine	________	________

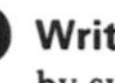
Writing Words by Syllables. Write each word your teacher dictates by syllables. Then write the whole word on the line provided.

	First Syllable	Second Syllable	Third Syllable	Fourth Syllable	Whole Word
1.	cur	dle			curdle
2.	ab	sor	bent		absorbent
3.	at	trac	tion		attraction
4.	con	fir	ma	tion	confirmation
5.	dis	ar	ma	ment	disarmament
6.	trans	for	ma	tion	transformation

Now write these five-syllable words:

7.	in	tel	lec	tu	al	intellectual
8.	sim	pli	fi	ca	tion	simplification

Use three of the words you wrote in sentences.

1. ________________________________
2. ________________________________
3. ________________________________

88 Lesson 17

4 Review of Syllable Types

If necessary, review the attributes of each of the syllable types students have studied before they begin this exercise.

5 Writing Words by Syllables

Dictate the words by syllables, emphasizing the syllables and having students write them on the lines provided. Then pronounce the whole word normally. Remind students that the number of blanks indicates the number of syllables in the word.

Don't be concerned about formal syllable divisions. In some of these words, the blends students have been studying are divided between syllables. If students write *ab sorb ent* instead of *ab sor bent*, for instance, accept their response. It is more important for them to spell the word correctly than to have their syllabication match that of the dictionary.

Additional Activities:

Have students look up the meanings of any of these words that they don't already know.

Have them use the rest of the words in original sentences.

6 **Using Words with Many Syllables.** Fill in the blanks in the sentences with the words listed below. Use each word only once.

aspirations	confirmation	difficulties
attraction	consultation	transformation

1. Did you receive a confirmation of your airline reservations?
2. The roller coaster is the main attraction at the amusement park.
3. Herb has aspirations toward becoming a professional baseball player.
4. Trudy has undergone a complete transformation since she started her exercise program.
5. Carl has a consultation with Dr. Jenkins tomorrow to discuss his operation.
6. The Campbells ran into a great many difficulties when they were remodeling their house.

7 **Dictionary Skills: Homonyms.** Use your dictionary to help you choose the correct word from each homonym pair in parentheses. Write the correct words on the lines provided.

1. Do you think Stan (heard/herd) what I said? heard
2. That old washcloth is all (warn/worn) out. worn
3. Herb is raising a (heard/herd) of sheep. herd
4. He played several (cords/chords) to try out the guitar. chords
5. Why did Frank (warn/worn) you not to go there? warn

8 **Writing Sentences.** On the lines below, write the sentences that you hear.

1. Norm dug up a rusty old sword down by the wharf.
2. Herb earns a paycheck while he is learning the job.
3. I've been told that the early bird catches the worm.
4. The farmer heard a word of warning from inside the barn.
5. Ronald sprinkled herbs on the surface of the warm roast.

Lesson 17 89

6 Using Words with Many Syllables

In this exercise, students complete sentences with some of the polysyllabic words that they have written by syllables in previous exercises.

7 Dictionary Skills: Homonyms

In this exercise, students select from a pair of homonyms the correct word based on context. Remind students that the spelling of a homonym is determined by its meaning in context. They should use their dictionaries to check the meaning of any word they aren't sure of.

8 Writing Sentences

Instruct students to write the sentences that you dictate, which are on the replica of the student page.

These sentences give students an opportunity to write the sight words and some of the representative words in context. Note any specific errors that students make, and design additional words, sentences, or phrases for specific problems.

In addition to the blends covered in this lesson, the patterns found in these sentences include:
—compound words (2)
—contractions (3)
—Silent *e* Pattern 1 (5)

Lesson 18

The Blends *rt*, *rl*, *rk*, *rse*, *rce*, and *rp*

Objectives

- **Blends:** Learn to spell words having the ending blends *rt*, *rl*, *rk*, *rse*, *rce*, and *rp*.
- **Sight Words:** Learn to spell *source*, *resource*, *pearl*, *corps*, *warp*, and *worse*. Use the sight words to complete sentences.
- **Patterns:** Review and practice using Silent *e* Patterns 1 and 2.
- **Alternative Spellings:** Learn that /rs/ at the end of words can be spelled *rce* or *rse* and that *rse* is the more common spelling.
- **Dictionary Skills:** Use the dictionary to determine the spelling of /rs/.
- **Homonyms:** Use designated homonyms in original sentences.
- **Writing Sentences:** Practice writing representative and sight words in context.
- **Puzzle:** Use representative words to complete a puzzle.

Lesson 18

The Blends *rt*, *rl*, *rk*, *rse*, *rce*, and *rp*

Sight Words		
source	pearl	warp
resource	corps	worse

Blends: *rt*, *rl*, *rk*, *rse*, *rce*, *rp*

1 Listening

Listen to the sound of *rt* in these words.

shirt	alert	port	part
skirt	expert	sport	quart
dirty	inverted	comfort	forty

Listen to the sound of *rl* in these words.

girl	curl	hurl
swirl	purl	whirl
twirling	unfurled	snarl

Listen to the sound of *rk* in these words.

dark	remark	fork	network
park	postmark	pork	housework

Listen to the sound of *rse* in these words.

coarse	verse	curse	sparse
course	reverse	nurses	endorse
horse	converse	purse	rehearse
hoarse	disperse	reimburse	discourse

Listen to the sound of *rce* in these words.

scarce	force	divorced	fierce
scarcely	enforce	reinforce	pierce

Listen to the sound of *rp* in these words.

burp	harp	sharp	chirping

90 Lesson 18

Sight Words

Teach the sight words using the methods described on pages 9-12 in the introduction to this book.

Note that these words all contain *r*-blends. Since they are also ending blends, they produce *r*-controlled vowels. Remind students that when *r* follows a vowel, it often signals an unpredictable vowel spelling.

Point out that both the *p* and the *s* are silent in the word *corps*.

1 Listening

As in Lesson 17, due to the difficulties involved in pronouncing *r*-controlled vowels and *r*-blends in isolation, we recommend the following variations in presenting the listening exercise.

1. Use a schwa with the blends when you pronounce them by themselves.
2. Attach the vowel to the blend when you separate individual words into their phonetic parts.

Introduce the words with the blend *rt* using the following steps.

1. Say the sound /ərt/ and ask students what letters make the sound. (Students reply *r-t*.)
2. Say the letters *r-t* and ask students what sound they make. (Students reply /ərt/.)
3. Say the word *shirt* and ask students what letters spell /sh/ and what letters spell /irt/.
4. Say the word *shirt* and ask students what letters spell *shirt*.

Follow the same steps to introduce the words with the blends *rl*, *rk*, *rse*, *rce*, and *rp*.

Draw students' attention to some of the words in which the same vowel sound is spelled differently, such as *shirt*/*alert*, *girl*/*curl*, and *verse*/*curse*.

Make sure that students know the meanings of all the representative words before going on with the lesson.

2 Writing Words. On the lines below, write the words that you hear.

1. girl	5. sharp	9. fierce
2. import	6. fork	10. postmark
3. forceful	7. twirled	11. adverse
4. quarter	8. reverse	12. endorsement

3 Using Sight Words. Use one of the sight words from this lesson to complete each sentence.

1. Jane has a string of pearls that belonged to her grandmother.
2. The U.S. Army Air Corps became the U.S. Air Force.
3. If managed, forests are a renewable natural resource.
4. Trees are a common source for the pulp used to make paper.
5. The patient is feeling worse today than he was yesterday.
6. If you let that wood get wet, it will warp.

4 Word Building with Silent *e* Patterns. Review Silent *e* Patterns 1 and 2 and then add the endings to the words below.

Pattern 1: The final silent *e* is dropped from a word when an ending that begins with a vowel is added.

Pattern 2: When an ending that begins with *a* or *o* is added to a word that ends in *ce* or *ge*, the silent *e* is kept to retain the soft *c* and *g* sounds.

1. scarce + ity	scarcity	7. enforce + able	enforceable
2. force + ing	forcing	8. reverse + ible	reversible
3. reverse + al	reversal	9. resource + ful	resourceful
4. fierce + ly	fiercely	10. pierce + ing	piercing
5. worse + en	worsen	11. nurse + ery	nursery
6. disperse + al	dispersal	12. reinforce + able	reinforceable

Lesson 18 91

2 Writing Words

Instruct students to write the words that you dictate, which are found on the replica of the student page. Say each word, use it in a phrase or simple sentence, and say the word again.

3 Using Sight Words

This exercise gives students additional practice in writing the sight words in this lesson by using them to complete sentences. Check to be sure students capitalize *corps* in number 2.

4 Word Building with Silent *e* Patterns

This exercise reviews Silent *e* Patterns 1 and 2. Remind students that in both patterns, the silent *e* is retained if the suffix begins with a consonant.

This exercise contrasts words ending in *ce* with those ending in *se* to make sure students understand Silent *e* Pattern 2, which applies only to words ending in *ce* and *ge*. Words ending in *se* follow Silent *e* Pattern 1. Check to be sure students have not retained the *e* in numbers 3 and 6.

5 Dictionary Skills: Finding the Correct Spelling. The sound /rs/ at the end of a word can be spelled *rce* or *rse*. Use the dictionary to find the correct spellings of the words spelled phonetically below. When you find the spelling that matches the meaning, write the word in the appropriate column.

Phonetic Spelling	Meaning	rce	rse
1. /ăd vŭrs′/	harmful; unfavorable; opposing		adverse
2. /fărs/	a ridiculous action or situation	farce	
3. /rē mŏrs′/	great regret		remorse
4. /tĕrs/	short and to the point		terse
5. /kŏm′ ərs/	the buying and selling of goods	commerce	
6. /dĭ vŭrs′/	distinctly different from each other		diverse
7. /dĭs bŭrs′/	to pay out from a fund		disburse
8. /ĭn vŭrs′/	reversed in order or effect		inverse

Notice how many words you wrote in each column. *Rse* is a more common spelling than *rce*. There are almost three times as many words spelled with *rse* as there are words spelled with *rce*.

6 Dictionary Skills: Homonyms. Use each of the homonyms below in a sentence. Look up the meanings in the dictionary if necessary.

1. coarse ____________________
2. course ____________________
3. hoarse ____________________
4. horse ____________________
5. core ____________________
6. corps ____________________

92 Lesson 18

5 Dictionary Skills: Finding the Correct Spelling

In this exercise, students determine the correct spelling of a sound that has alternative spellings. Remind students that the phonetic spelling represents the way the word is pronounced. If students have trouble finding number 5 in their dictionaries, remind them that /k/ can be spelled either *c* or *k*. Point out that English words beginning with *ko* are very rare.

When students have completed this exercise, review with them some of the strategies they have learned for selecting the correct spelling when there are alternative spellings for the same sound combination. These strategies include creating a mental picture of the spelling of a word, developing a mnemonic device for a troublesome word, selecting the most probable spelling, and using the dictionary. Point out that *rse* is the more probable spelling for /rs/ because there are more words spelled with *rse* than with *rce*.

Additional Activity:

For students who are adept at using probabilities to predict spellings, you may want to contrast the *rce/rse* endings with the *nce/nse* endings. *Rse* is the more common spelling for /rs/. But *nce* is a far more common spelling for /ns/ because so many words are formed with the *ance/ence* suffixes. Use your own judgment on whether or not to point this out to students. It may help some students but confuse others.

6 Dictionary Skills: Homonyms

The homonyms *coarse* and *course* were first encountered in Book 2 and are reviewed here. Students will probably be familiar with some of the other homonyms as well, so they won't have to look up the definitions. However, they should look up any they are unsure of. Stress the fact that knowing the meaning of the word is the only sure way of spelling a homonym correctly.

7 Writing Sentences. On the lines below, write the sentences that you hear.

1. I heard that Mark gave his girlfriend a pearl ring.
2. It was hard to stay alert after working forty hours.
3. Rain forests are the source of many important resources.
4. Robert has been in the Marine Corps for twenty-one years.
5. My attempt to straighten the warped board made it worse.
6. Have the actors started to rehearse their parts in the play?

8 Puzzle. Use the clues below to fill in the blocks of the puzzle. All of the answers are representative words or sight words in this lesson. When you have filled in all the correct answers, the shaded blocks will spell a new word ending in *rse*.

Clues

Clue	Answer
1. to throw something with force	H U R L
2. to add strength to something	R E I N F O R C E
3. to make a hole in something	P I E R C E
4. turn backward or change direction	R E V E R S E
5. turned upside down	I N V E R T E D
6. rough; not smooth or fine	C O A R S E
7. the origin or beginning of something	S O U R C E
8. a highly skilled person	E X P E R T

The new word: UNIVERSE

On the line below, write a sentence using the new word.

____

Lesson 18 93

7 Writing Sentences

Instruct students to write the sentences that you dictate, which are on the replica of the student page.

These sentences give students an opportunity to write the sight words and some of the representative words in context. Note any specific errors that students make, and design additional words, sentences, or phrases for specific problems.

Make sure students have capitalized *Marine Corps* in sentence 4.

In addition to the blends covered in this lesson, the patterns found in these sentences include:
—possessive pronouns (1, 5, and 6)
—compound words (1)
—hyphenated numbers (4)

8 Puzzle

Have students complete the puzzle by writing each answer word in the blocks next to the clue. If necessary, give them the following list of answer words.

coarse	pierce
expert	reinforce
hurl	reverse
inverted	source

When students have completed the puzzle, the word *universe* will be spelled vertically in the shaded blocks. Have students write this word on the line provided and use it in an original sentence.

Review of Unit 5

Blends That End Syllables

Objectives

- **Word Building:** Add ending blends to word parts to form words.
- **Suffixes:** Review the alternative spellings for /shən/ and strategies for predicting the spellings. Fill in the correct spellings to complete words.
- **Pattern:** Review Silent *e* Pattern 2 and follow it to form words.
- **Comparisons:** Review forming comparatives and superlatives and write dictated phrases containing them.
- **Compound Words:** Match words to form compound words.
- **Alternative Spellings:** Write dictated phrases containing /ld/ and /kt/.
  Fill in *rce* or *rse* to spell words in context.
- **Homonyms:** Select the correct spelling of homonyms based on context.
- **Root Words:** Identify root words by removing prefixes and suffixes.
- **Writing Sentences:** Practice writing representative and sight words in context.
- **Composing Sentences:** Write original sentences using representative and sight words.
- **Puzzle:** Review representative and sight words by completing a crossword puzzle.

Review of Unit 5

Blends That End Syllables

1 Word Building. Write one of the blends below in each blank to make a word. Do not make the same word twice.

mp st sp sk lt ld lm lk lp lf ct ft pt xt

1. ba_ld_	8. exa_ct_	15. ne_xt_
2. ba_sk_	9. gra_ft_	16. ne_st_
3. cla_sp_	10. he_lp_	17. pa_ct_
4. cra_ft_	11. he_lm_	18. sta_mp_
5. cre_pt_	12. hu_mp_	19. ti_lt_
6. cru_st_	13. ke_pt_	20. wa_sp_
7. de_sk_	14. mi_lk_	21. wo_lf_

2 Spelling Words That End in /shən/. Answer the questions below.

1. Write three ways you have learned to spell /shən/ at the end of words.
   tion _sion_ _cian_
2. What is the most common spelling of /shən/? _tion_
3. When the root verb ends in *ct* or *pt*, _ion_ is added to form the noun.
4. When you hear /k/ or /p/ before /shən/ at the end of a word, how will the /shən/ be spelled? _tion_

Write the correct spelling of /shən/ on the lines below.

1. attrac_tion_	4. adop_tion_	7. admis_sion_
2. recep_tion_	5. musi_cian_	8. connec_tion_
3. profes_sion_	6. infec_tion_	9. discus_sion_

94 Review of Unit 5

1 Word Building

Have students add one of the ending blends to each word part to make a word. Encourage them to use all of the ending blends at least once. The answers given on the replica of the student page are examples. Many other combinations are possible. Accept all correctly spelled words.

2 Spelling Words That End in /shən/

The first part of this exercise reviews some of the strategies for determining the spelling of /shən/ at the end of words. Then students must fill in the correct spelling of /shən/ to complete each given word. Remind students that each word ends in /shən/ and that they should say each word to themselves before deciding how the suffix is spelled.

3 **Review of Silent *e* Pattern 2.** Fill in the blanks to complete the pattern below.

Pattern: When an ending that begins with _a_ or _o_ is added to a word that ends in *ce* or *ge*, the silent *e* is kept to retain the soft _c_ and _g_ sounds.

Add the endings to the words below. Keep the silent *e* when necessary.

1. enforce + able _enforceable_
2. force + ible _forcible_
3. pierce + ing _piercing_
4. outrage + ous _outrageous_
5. dance + ing _dancing_
6. reverse + al _reversal_
7. reverse + ible _reversible_
8. fierce + ly _fiercely_
9. entrance + ing _entrancing_
10. recharge + able _rechargeable_

4 **Review of the *-er* and *-est* Suffixes.** The suffixes *-er* and *-est* are added to adjectives and adverbs to show comparison. Fill in the blanks below to review how they are used.

1. The *-er* ending is used when _two_ things are being compared.
2. The *-est* ending is used when _three_ or more things are being compared.
3. *-Er* and *-est* are usually added to words of _one_ or _two_ syllables.
4. The words _more_ and _most_ are usually used with words of three or more syllables to show comparison.

Write the phrases you hear on the lines below.

1. the boldest soldier
2. a stormier night
3. the silkiest cloth
4. the darker uniforms
5. the curliest hair
6. the fiercest storm
7. the sharpest object
8. the more dangerous sport
9. the saltier crackers
10. the judge's strictest verdict

Review of Unit 5 95

3 Review of Silent *e* Pattern 2

This exercise reviews Silent *e* Pattern 2 and gives students additional practice with it. Students may fill in the phonetic spellings, i.e. /s/ and /j/, rather than the letters *c* and *g* to complete the pattern. Accept this as a correct response.

Check to be sure students retain the silent *e* in numbers 1, 4, 8, and 10, and not in the others.

4 Review of the *-er* and *-est* Suffixes

This exercise reviews the patterns for using *-er*, *-est*, *more*, and *most* to show comparisons. When students have finished the first part of the exercise, dictate the phrases found on the replica of the student page. Remind students to follow the patterns they have studied for adding endings.

5 Word Building: Compound Words. Match a word from Column 2 with each word in Column 1 to make a compound word. Use each word in Column 1 only once. Check your dictionary to find whether the compounds are closed, hyphenated, or open.

Column 1	Column 2	Compound Words	
adult	bird	1. adulthood	9. leftover
folk	boiled		
fore	burly	2. folk singer	10. next door
ghost	cellar		
hard	craft	3. foreword	11. silkworm
heart	door		
help	felt	4. ghost town	12. songbird
hurly	fish		
left	hood	5. hard-boiled	13. spacecraft
next	mate		
silk	over	6. heartfelt	14. storm cellar
song	pike		
space	singer	7. helpmate	15. swordfish
storm	town		
sword	word	8. hurly-burly	16. turnpike
turn	worm		

6 Alternative Spellings for /ld/ and /kt/. Write the phrases you hear.

1. elect a president
2. a stacked deck
3. bowled a game
4. attacked by bees
5. build a barn
6. jacked up the car
7. inspect the package
8. enrolled in the course

7 Reviewing Homonyms. Select the correct word in each sentence and write it on the line provided.

1. Of (coarse/course) Frank can fix your fence. course
2. You'll have to tie that package with strong (chord/cord). cord
3. Have you (heard/herd) the news? heard
4. Did you (warn/worn) him not to go into the street? warn
5. Clark's cold made his voice (hoarse/horse). hoarse

96 Review of Unit 5

5 Word Building: Compound Words

In this exercise, students build compound words by matching each word in column 1 with a word from column 2. The words on the replica of the student page are examples. A few more combinations are possible. Accept all compound words that are listed in a dictionary.

Remind students that all dictionaries may not agree on whether a compound is closed, hyphenated, or open. You may also want to point out that a compound may be written more than one way, depending on how it is used in a sentence. For instance, *next door* is open when it is a noun but hyphenated when it is an adjective, as in *next-door neighbor*. Mention this only if it will clear up confusion, not if you think it will create confusion.

6 Alternative Spellings for /ld/ and /kt/

Before beginning this exercise, review the alternative spellings for /ld/ (*ld* and *lled*) and /kt/ (*ct* and *cked*). Then dictate the phrases found on the replica of the student page.

7 Reviewing Homonyms

If students have any trouble completing this exercise, review the meanings of the various homonyms with them.

8 **Word Building: Alternative Spellings for /rs/.** Fill in the blanks in the sentences below with *rse* or *rce*. Remember that *rse* is the more common spelling.

1. If you will endo_r_ _s_ _e_ this check, I'll deposit it.
2. A referee's job is to enfo_r_ _c_ _e_ the rules of the game.
3. As soon as I got to the doctor's office, a nu_r_ _s_ _e_ took my temperature.
4. Fred forgot the third ve_r_ _s_ _e_ of the song he was singing.
5. There was a very spa_r_ _s_ _e_ crowd at the fair because of the rain.
6. Did Mr. Wolf reimbu_r_ _s_ _e_ you for the money you spent fixing his faucet?
7. My grandmother used to say things were "as sca_r_ _c_ _e_ as hen's teeth."
8. Grandmother also used to say, "You can lead a ho_r_ _s_ _e_ to water, but you can't make him drink."

9 **Finding Root Words.** Write the root word for each word below.

1. comfortable	comfort	6. transformation	form *or* transform
2. adaptation	adapt	7. conversation	converse
3. disarmament	arm *or* disarm	8. consultation	consult
4. unfurled	furl	9. expectation	expect
5. costliest	cost *or* costly	10. unselfishness	self *or* selfish

10 **Writing Sentences.** On the lines below, write the sentences that you hear.

1. Herb's best sports are basketball and golf.
2. Clark suspected that the new rules were unenforceable.
3. Bert ran into difficulty when he repaired his surfboard.
4. Donald's reaction to the interruption was swift.
5. While I was working on a hoist at the wharf last summer, a fierce storm blew up without warning.

Review of Unit 5 97

8 Word Building: Alternative Spellings for /rs/

This exercise reviews the spelling of words that end in /rs/. All of the /rs/ words were representative words in Lesson 18, so students should have little trouble completing it.

9 Finding Root Words

In this exercise, students can see the relationsip between a word and the root word from which it was built. You may decide to allow *disarm*, *costly*, *transform*, and *selfish* as answers to numbers 3, 5, 6, and 10. However, if you do accept these as correct answers, discuss the fact that these words contain root words as well.

10 Writing Sentences

Instruct students to write the sentences that you dictate, which are on the replica of the student page.

These sentences give students an opportunity to write some of the representative words and sight words from this unit in context. Note any specific errors that students make, and design additional words, sentences, or phrases for specific problems.

In addition to the blends covered in this unit, the patterns found in these sentences include:
—compound words (1 and 3)
—possessives (1 and 4)
—Silent *e* Pattern 2 (2)
—possessive pronouns (3)
—words ending in /shən/ (4)

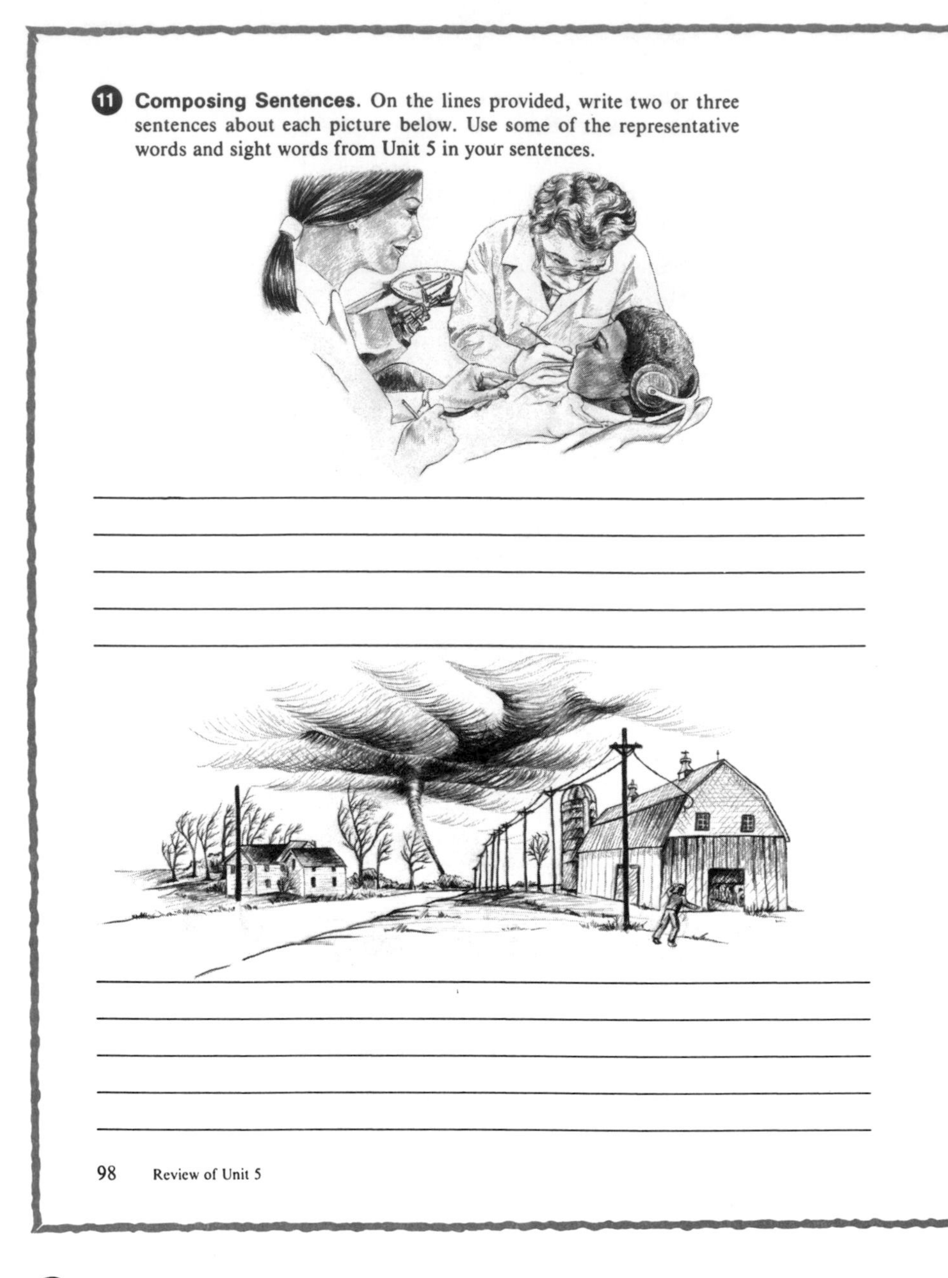

11 Composing Sentences. On the lines provided, write two or three sentences about each picture below. Use some of the representative words and sight words from Unit 5 in your sentences.

98 Review of Unit 5

11 Composing Sentences

Discuss the illustrations with students before they begin to write their sentences. You might also have them look through the word lists for Unit 5 representative and sight words that they could use.

Encourage students to look up words they aren't sure of after they have finished writing. Remember that errors in words that haven't been studied yet shouldn't be treated negatively. Point out any parts of the word that are spelled correctly and praise the effort.

 **Crossword Puzzle.** Use the clues below to complete this crossword puzzle. Most of the answers are representative words or sight words from Unit 5 or contain Unit 5 blends.

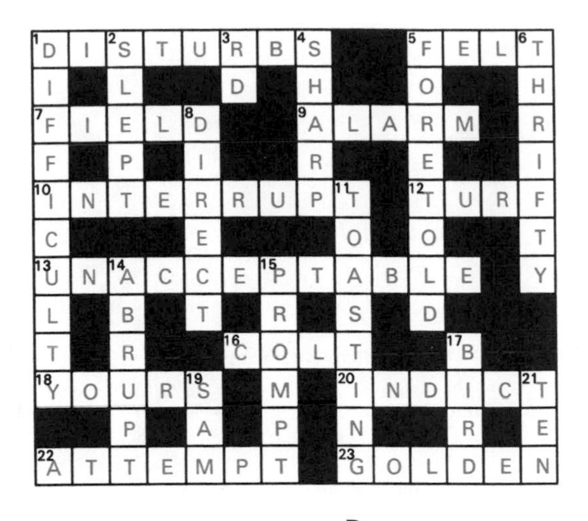

Across

1. Bothers; annoys: ___ the peace
5. Past tense of feel
7. A place for growing crops
9. A warning sound; a signal
10. To break into a conversation
12. Grassy soil; sod
13. Not good enough to be approved
16. A young horse
18. A possessive personal pronoun
20. To accuse of a crime
22. Try
23. A yellowish color

Down

1. A problem or hardship; something that must be overcome
2. Was asleep
3. Abbreviation for road
4. Opposite of dull; a ___ knife
5. Predicted; forecast
6. Careful about money
8. Give orders or directions
11. Browning bread or marshmallows
14. Sudden; all at once
15. On time
17. An animal that can fly
19. Short for Samuel
21. Five plus five

12 Crossword Puzzle

Have students complete the crossword puzzle. Tell them that most of the answer words are representative or sight words from Unit 5. The clues are mostly definitions that rely on the students' general knowledge.

Allow them to use a dictionary if they want to. You might want them to work in pairs or small groups. If necessary, give them the following list of answer words and have them check off words as they use them.

abrupt
alarm
attempt
bird
colt
difficulty
direct
disturbs
felt
field
foretold
golden
indict
interrupt
prompt
Rd.
Sam
sharp
slept
ten
thrifty
toasting
turf
unacceptable
yours

Unit 5 Tests

We recommend that you test your students on the representative words and sight words from Unit 5 before going on. The following are suggested lists of representative words and sight words from Unit 5. You may want to substitute other words to meet the needs of your students.

Dictate each word and use it in a simple sentence. Students should be able to spell 90 percent of these words correctly.

Representative Words	Sight Words
1. desk	1. moist
2. company	2. worth
3. left	3. clerk
4. comfort	4. bought
5. perfect	5. captain
6. slept	6. forth
7. reverse	7. soldier
8. turn	8. word
9. girl	9. ghost
10. adult	10. earn
11. disturb	11. work
12. storm	12. resource
13. sharpest	13. pearl
14. film	14. world
15. postmark	15. sword
16. rebuild	16. corps
17. helpless	17. personal
18. selfish	18. example
19. reinforce	19. personnel
20. third	20. listen

Lesson 19

The Silent Partners *mb*, *mn*, *lm*, and *lk*

Objectives

- **Silent Partners:** Learn to spell words with the silent partners *mb, mn, lm*, and *lk*.
- **Sight Words:** Learn to spell *psalm*, *often*, *soften*, *softener*, *wherever*, and *threshold*.
- **Silent Consonants:** Identify the silent consonant in the consonant pairs in this lesson and learn that both consonants in these pairs are pronounced in some words.
- **Dictionary Skills:** Learn the "related words" strategy for remembering the silent consonant in certain words.
- **Composing Sentences:** Write original sentences using silent-consonant and related words.
- **Mnemonics:** Learn that mnemonic devices can aid in remembering the silent consonant in words and develop some mnemonics for troublesome words.
- **Writing Sentences:** Practice writing representative and sight words in context.

Sight Words

Teach the sight words using the methods described on pages 9-12 in the introduction to this book.

Point out the silent *p* in *psalm* and the silent *t* in *soften* and *softener*. In the preferred pronunciation of *often*, the *t* is silent, also. It is acceptable to pronounce the *t*, however.

Note that when *where* and *ever* are combined to form one word, the silent *e* on *where* is dropped. Normally when compound words are formed, no letters in either word are dropped or changed. Point out that there is only one *h* in the middle of *threshold.*

Lesson 19

The Silent Partners *mb*, *mn*, *lm*, and *lk*

Sight Words		
psalm	soften	wherever
often	softener	threshold

Silent Partners

1 Listening

mb — Listen to the sound of *mb* in these words.

lamb	comb	numb	dumb
limb	womb	crumb	dumbwaiter
climb	bombshell	plumber	thumbnail

mn — Listen to the sound of *mn* in these words.

hymn	column	condemn
autumn	solemn	condemned

lm — Listen to the sound of *lm* in these words.

calm	balm	qualm
palm	embalm	Malcolm

lk — Listen to the sound of *lk* in these words.

talk	walk	folk	yolk
stalk	crosswalk	folklore	chalk

Underline the silent consonants in the representative words above.

1 Listening

This unit deals with consonant pairs and clusters that contain a silent consonant. We refer to these consonant pairs as "silent partners" to remind students that although they only hear one sound, two consonants are needed to spell the sound in words that contain silent partners.

Introduce the words with the silent partners *mb* using the following steps.

1. Say the sound /m/ and ask students what letters spell the sound in these representative words. Emphasize that the *b* is part of what spells the sound. It is the silent partner.
2. Say the letters *m-b* and ask students what sound they spell.
3. Say the word *lamb* and ask students what letters spell /la/ and what letters spell /mb/.
4. Say the word *lamb* and ask students what letters spell *lamb*.

Point out that the pronunciation of the vowel varies among words with the same spelling, i.e., *limb*/*climb* and *comb*/*womb*/*bomb*.

Follow the same steps to introduce the words with the silent partners *mn*, *lm*, and *lk*.

2 Writing Words. On the lines below, write the words that you hear.

1. climb	5. combing	9. condemn
2. calmest	6. balmy	10. cornstalk
3. chalk	7. solemn	11. plumber
4. hymn	8. thumb	12. boardwalk

3 Silent Consonants. Sometimes when *mb*, *mn*, *lm*, and *lk* occur in words, one consonant in each pair is silent. In some words, both consonants can be heard.

Underline the silent consonants in the words below. If all the consonants can be heard, underline the whole word. Use your dictionary to check the pronunciation, if necessary.

mb	mn	lm	lk
1. mumble	6. condemn	11. elm	16. balk
2. succumb	7. dimness	12. palm	17. silky
3. tomb	8. autumn	13. film	18. talking
4. climber	9. chimney	14. helmet	19. bulkier
5. September	10. warmness	15. calmness	20. chalky

Now fill in the blanks below.

1. If one consonant is silent in the pair *mb*, it is usually the b.
2. If one consonant is silent in the pair *mn*, it is usually the n.
3. If one consonant is silent in the pair *lm*, it is usually the l.
4. If one consonant is silent in the pair *lk*, it is usually the l.

In some regions of the country, the *l* in some of the *lm* words is slightly pronounced. If students do pronounce the *l* in these words, explain that in some regions this letter is silent. Students who do pronounce the *l* will find it easier to spell these words, of course.

When all of the representative words have been introduced, have students underline the silent consonants.

Make sure that students know the meanings of all the representative words before going on with the lesson.

2 Writing Words

Instruct students to write the words that you dictate, which are found on the replica of the student page. Say each word, use it in a phrase or simple sentence, and say the word again.

3 Silent Consonants

This exercise draws students' attention to the fact that the consonant pairs in this lesson do not always contain a silent consonant. Suggest that students pronounce the words aloud if they have trouble deciding whether or not a word contains a silent consonant. It is important for students to know that both consonants in these consonant pairs are often pronounced.

Additional Activity:

Have students think of other words that contain these consonant pairs in which both consonants are pronounced.

4 Dictionary Skills: Silent Consonants. Some words that contain a silent consonant have related words in which that consonant is pronounced. Learning these words can help you to remember the silent consonant in the root or related word.

Look up the word *columnist* in the dictionary. Write the pronunciation and meaning below.

columnist /kŏl′ əm nĭst/ a person who writes a column in a newspaper or magazine

Remembering the word *columnist* can help you remember the silent *n* in the word *column.*

Now look up the words below in your dictionary. For each word, find a related word in which the silent consonant is pronounced. Write the related words and their meanings on the lines provided.

	Related Word	Meaning
1. autumn	autumnal	of or like autumn
2. hymn	hymnal	a book of collected hymns
3. bomb	bombard	to attack with bombs or shells
4. crumb	crumble	to break into small pieces or fall apart
5. soften	soft	not hard; not loud; mild, gentle
6. condemn	condemnation	the act of condemning
7. solemn	solemnity	a serious or solemn ceremony

Now choose three pairs of silent-consonant and related words and use each of the pairs in a sentence. See the example below.

Example: *Autumn* begins with the *autumnal* equinox.

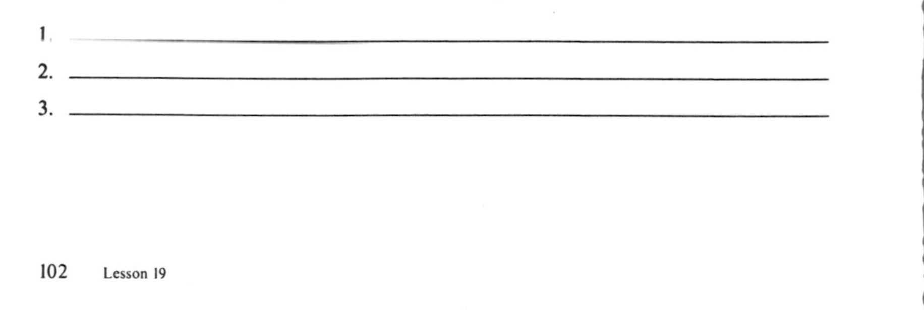

1. ________
2. ________
3. ________

102 Lesson 19

4 Dictionary Skills: Silent Consonants

This exercise introduces a strategy for remembering the silent letter in some words. This is called the "related words" strategy. When students have looked up *columnist* and written their definitions, discuss the fact that some words that contain a silent consonant have a related word in which that consonant is heard.

Before students begin to look up related words for the seven words listed in the exercise, explain that the related word may be listed as an entry word, but it may also be listed at the end of the entry for the given word. For instance, *autumnal* may be listed as the adjective form of *autumn*, and *condemnation* may be listed as the noun form of *condemn.* In this case, the related word will not be defined, and you may have to help students generate a definition.

The answers given on the replica of the student page are examples. For most of the words there are other equally acceptable related words. Encourage students to write the definitions in their own words.

If students have trouble writing the sentences at the end of the exercise, give them one or two more examples, such as "There are many *hymns* in the *hymnal*" or "The cookie *crumbled* into many *crumbs.*" You might want to do this part of the exercise as a group activity. These sentences will help prepare students for the exercise on mnemonics which follows.

 **Mnemonics.** Look up the word *mnemonic* in your dictionary. Write the pronunciation and the definition on the lines below.

mnemonic /nĭ mŏn′ ĭk/ a device used to assist the memory, such as a rhyme or a formula

Mnemonics help us to remember things. For instance, you can distinguish between the homonyms *here* and *hear* if you remember that *hear* has the word *ear* in it.

Mnemonics can also help you to remember how to spell words that contain silent consonants. These mnemonics can be either phrases or sentences that link the silent-consonant word with a word you know how to spell.

Example: *Dumbo* was not a *dumb* elephant.

The best mnemonics are ones that you develop yourself. Make up mnemonics for any of the following words that you have trouble spelling.

1. climb — You must be limber to climb out on that limb.
2. palm — My pal gave me that palm.
3. numb — Those numbers left him numb.
4. plumber — The plumber found lumber in the water tank.
5. limb — He kept his limbs limber with daily exercise.
6. thumb — He pinched his thumb between two pieces of lumber.
7. stalk — Stalk = s + talk

6 Writing Sentences. On the lines below, write the sentences that you hear.

1. We often take walks on balmy autumn afternoons.
2. Many of the hymns in the hymnal are based on psalms.
3. Fran adds a softener to the rinse to soften the clothes.
4. We climbed the steps and walked across the threshold.
5. Wherever Malcolm went, he collected the local folklore.

Lesson 19 103

5 Mnemonics

This exercise presents another strategy for remembering the spelling of difficult words. After students have looked up the pronunciation and meaning of *mnemonics*, discuss the concept with them. Remind them of some of the mnemonic devices they are familiar with, such as the "Thirty days have September, April, June, and November" rhyme for remembering the number of days in each month. Ask them about their favorite methods for remembering things. Do they tie a string around a finger? Wear a ring on an unaccustomed finger? Write notes to themselves? Put something in a conspicuous place?

This exercise emphasizes the fact that mnemonics work best if they are developed by the individual. Some students will have a knack for this, while others will have some difficulty. Do not insist that everyone develop mnemonics for the given words. If your students have a lot of difficulty with this activity, do some or all of these as a group.

The examples on the replica of the student page are included to help your group get started. Notice that the sentence for number 1 could also be used for number 5.

6 Writing Sentences

Instruct students to write the sentences that you dictate, which are found on the replica of the student page.

Give students a bit more time to write these sentences than you normally do for dictations. They contain several silent partner words which may take students longer to recall.

These sentences give students an opportunity to write the sight words and some of the representative words in context. Note any specific errors that students make, and design additional words, sentences, or phrases for specific problems.

In addition to the silent partners covered in this lesson, the patterns found in these sentences include:
—compound words (1 and 5)
—Silent *e* Pattern 1 (2)
—related words strategy (2)

Lesson 20

The Silent Partners *gn*, *kn*, *wr*, and *stle*

Objectives

- **Silent Partners:** Learn to spell words with the silent partners *gn*, *kn*, *wr*, and *stle*.
- **Sight Words:** Learn to spell *reign*, *foreign*, *Lincoln*, *isle*, *aisle*, and *island*.
- **Silent Consonants:** Identify the silent consonants in the consonant pairs in this lesson and learn where these pairs are likely to occur in syllables.
- **Dictionary Skills:** Practice the related words strategy with designated words.
- **Mnemonics:** Develop mnemonics for troublesome words.
- **Homonyms:** Select the correct spelling of homonyms based on context.
- **Alternative Spellings:** Learn that /səl/ at the end of words can be spelled three ways and that *stle* is the most common spelling.
- **Dictionary Skills:** Use the dictionary to determine the correct spelling of /səl/ based on meaning.
- **Writing Sentences:** Practice writing representative and sight words in context.

Sight Words

Teach the sight words using the methods described on pages 9-12 in the introduction to this book.

Point out the silent consonants in these words. Help students to decide what strategies to use to remember the silent letters.

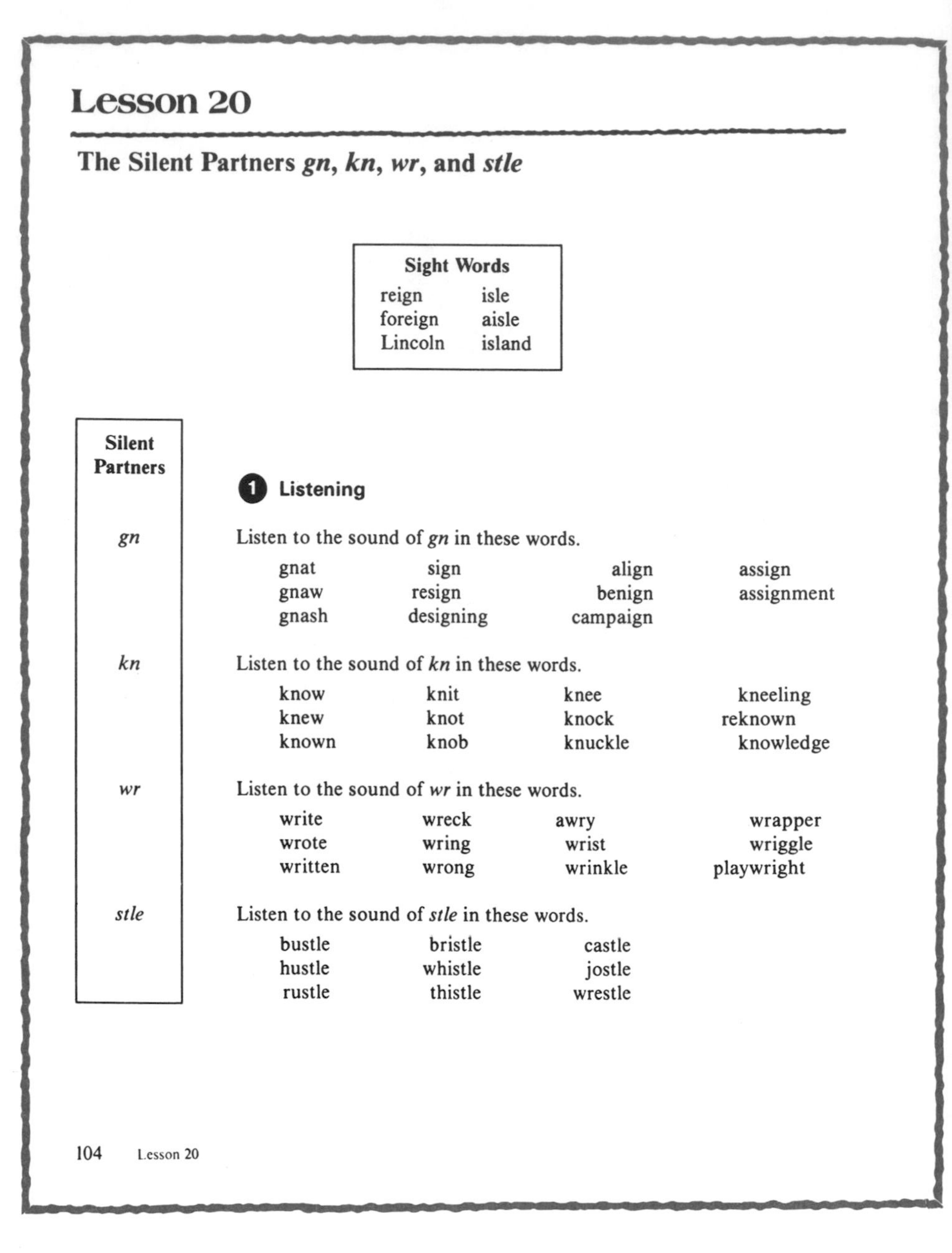

Lesson 20

The Silent Partners *gn*, *kn*, *wr*, and *stle*

Sight Words	
reign	isle
foreign	aisle
Lincoln	island

Silent Partners: *gn*, *kn*, *wr*, *stle*

1 Listening

Listen to the sound of *gn* in these words.

gnat	sign	align	assign
gnaw	resign	benign	assignment
gnash	designing	campaign	

Listen to the sound of *kn* in these words.

know	knit	knee	kneeling
knew	knot	knock	reknown
known	knob	knuckle	knowledge

Listen to the sound of *wr* in these words.

write	wreck	awry	wrapper
wrote	wring	wrist	wriggle
written	wrong	wrinkle	playwright

Listen to the sound of *stle* in these words.

bustle	bristle	castle
hustle	whistle	jostle
rustle	thistle	wrestle

104 Lesson 20

1 Listening

Introduce the words with the silent partners *gn* using the following steps.

1. Say the sound /n/ and ask students what letters spell the sound in these representative words. Emphasize that both letters are needed to spell the sound in these words.
2. Say the letters *g-n* and ask students what sound they spell.
3. Say the word *gnat* and ask students what letters spell /n/ and what letters spell /at/.
4. Say the word *gnat* and ask students what letters spell *gnat*.

Follow the same steps to introduce the words with the silent partners *kn*, *wr*, and *stle*.

Draw attention to *playwright*. Contrast the spelling of the suffix *-wright* with the spelling of the word *write*.

Make sure that students know the meanings of all the representative words before going on with the lesson.

2 Writing Words. On the lines below, write the words that you hear.

1. wrist	5. assign	9. rewrapped
2. knife	6. wrinkled	10. design
3. gnawing	7. whistle	11. knotted
4. bustled	8. knowledge	12. wrestle

3 Silent Consonants. Usually when the consonant pairs in this lesson occur in words, one consonant of each pair is silent. Pronounce each word in Exercise 1 and underline each silent consonant. Then fill in the blanks in the statements below.

1. In the consonant pair *gn*, the consonant g is usually silent.
2. In the consonant pair *kn*, the consonant k is usually silent.
3. In the consonant pair *wr*, the consonant w is usually silent.
4. In the group *stle*, the consonant t is usually silent.
5. The consonant pair gn occurs at both the beginning and end of syllables.
6. The consonant pairs kn and wr occur only at the beginning of syllables.

4 Dictionary Skills: Silent Consonants. In Lesson 19 you learned that some words that contain a silent consonant have related words in which that consonant is pronounced. These related words can help you remember the silent consonant in the root word. Look up the words below. For each word, find a related word in which the silent consonant is pronounced. Write the related words and their meanings on the lines provided.

	Related Word	Meaning
1. sign	signal	a sign or gesture that communicates meaning
2. design	designate	to indicate or specify; to appoint
3. malign	malignant	very harmful or injurious; evil
4. resign	resignation	the act of resigning

Lesson 20 105

2 Writing Words

Instruct students to write the words that you dictate, which are found on the replica of the student page. Say each word, use it in a phrase or simple sentence, and say the word again.

3 Silent Consonants

The primary purpose of this exercise is to draw students' attention to the silent letters in the consonant pairs *gn*, *kn*, and *wr*, and the cluster *stle* by having them underline the silent consonants in the representative words in Exercise 1.

Some of these representative words contain other silent consonants, however. Use your own judgment to decide whether or not to pursue this with your students. Students who have a great deal of difficulty with these words may simply be frustrated by having to find all of the silent letters in them.

On the other hand, students who are developing an interest in words may enjoy the challenge. For instance, they may enjoy noting that in words with double letters, only one letter is usually heard, and that the *w* in words like *gnaw*, *know*, *knew*, and *known* is not sounded, although it does affect the pronunciation of the vowel.

Regardless of how you decide to handle these other silent consonants, you should expect students to underline the *w* in *wrestle* as well as the *t*, and you can probably expect most students to identify the *gh* in *playwright* as being silent, as well.

4 Dictionary Skills: Silent Consonants

In this exercise, students review the related words strategy and apply it to some of the words in this lesson. The answers given on the replica of the student page are examples. There are other equally acceptable words, such as *signature* for *sign*.

5 Mnemonics. Mnemonics can be useful devices for remembering words that you have a great deal of trouble spelling. But you should develop mnemonics only when you really need them. Select four or five words from this lesson that you have trouble spelling and try to create mnemonics for them. Use the lines below.

	Word	Mnemonic
1.	____________	________________________________
2.	____________	________________________________
3.	____________	________________________________
4.	____________	________________________________
5.	____________	________________________________

6 Dictionary Skills: Homonyms. Many words with silent letters have homonyms that are spelled differently. The meaning of the word in context will determine the correct spelling. Answer the questions below using a dictionary to check the meanings of the homonyms when necessary.

1. Is the passageway in a theater an *aisle* or an *isle*? aisle
2. Do you *knead* or *need* the bread dough? knead
3. Is a recent purchase *knew* or *new*? new
4. Did you *knot* or *not* the string? knot
5. Do you *know* or *no* how to do that puzzle? know
6. Did King Arthur *rain* or *reign* long ago? reign
7. Do you *rap* or *wrap* a package? wrap
8. Did the army *rest* or *wrest* power from the king? wrest
9. Did the garbage *reek* or *wreak*? reek
10. Did you *ring* or *wring* out the laundry? wring
11. Was the bell *rung* or *wrung*? rung
12. Did you *rack* or *wrack* your brains for the answers? wrack

106 Lesson 20

5 Mnemonics

This exercise provides students with a chance to practice more mnemonics.

If your students have a great deal of difficulty developing mnemonics, you may want to do this as a group activity. Humor often works well in developing mnemonics. A silly saying will sometimes stick in the mind a long time.

6 Dictionary Skills: Homonyms

Students will probably be familiar with some of these homonyms, so they won't have to look up all of the definitions. However, they should look up any they are unsure of. Stress the fact that the meaning of the word in context determines the correct spelling of a homonym.

7 Dictionary Skills: Alternative Spellings for /səl/. When a word ends in /səl/, it sounds like it ends in a Cle syllable. However, very few /səl/ words are spelled with *sle* at the end. Look up the words spelled phonetically below to find three different ways to spell /səl/. Write each word in the appropriate column below.

1. /vĕs' əl/ a ship or large boat; a blood ____
2. /tŭs' əl/ a rough struggle
3. /ĕ pĭs' əl/ a long, formal letter
4. /chĭz' əl/ a tool used to shape wood, stone, or metal
5. /hăs' əl/ an argument or something troublesome
6. /grĭs' əl/ a tough, stringy material that makes meat hard to chew
7. /pĕs' əl/ a tool used for pounding or crushing something into powder
8. /tĭn' səl/ glittering bits of foil or metal used for decorations
9. /trĕs' əl/ a framework used to support railroad tracks or a road

stle	sel	sle
epistle	vessel	tussle
gristle	chisel	hassle
pestle	tinsel	
trestle		

The most common way to spell /səl/ at the end of a word is *stle*.

8 Writing Sentences. On the lines below, write the sentences that you hear.

1. Which playwright wrote about the reign of King Arthur?
2. That assignment calls for knowledge of foreign affairs.
3. The bride's dress rustled as she walked down the aisle.
4. Robert is writing about being shipwrecked on an island.
5. The Clarks go to the Isle of Palms to get away from the hustle and bustle of city life.
6. Lincoln wrestled with many problems throughout his campaign to become president.

Lesson 20 107

7 Dictionary Skills: Alternative Spellings for /səl/

This exercise draws students' attention to the fact that /səl/ at the end of a word can be spelled *stle*, *sel*, or *sle*. Emphasize the fact that *stle* is the most common spelling and *sle* is the least common.

Additional Activity:

Have students use some of these words in sentences of their own.

8 Writing Sentences

Instruct students to write the sentences that you dictate, which are on the replica of the student page. Give students a bit more time to write these sentences than you normally do for dictations. They contain several silent-partner words which may take students longer to recall.

These sentences give students an opportunity to write the sight words and some of the representative words in context. Note any specific errors that students make, and design additional words, sentences, or phrases for specific problems.

In addition to the silent partners covered in this lesson, the patterns found in these sentences include:
—compound words (1, 4, and 6)
—homonyms (1, 3, and 5)
—Silent *e* Pattern 1 (3, 4, and 6)
—possessives (3)
—possessive pronouns (6)

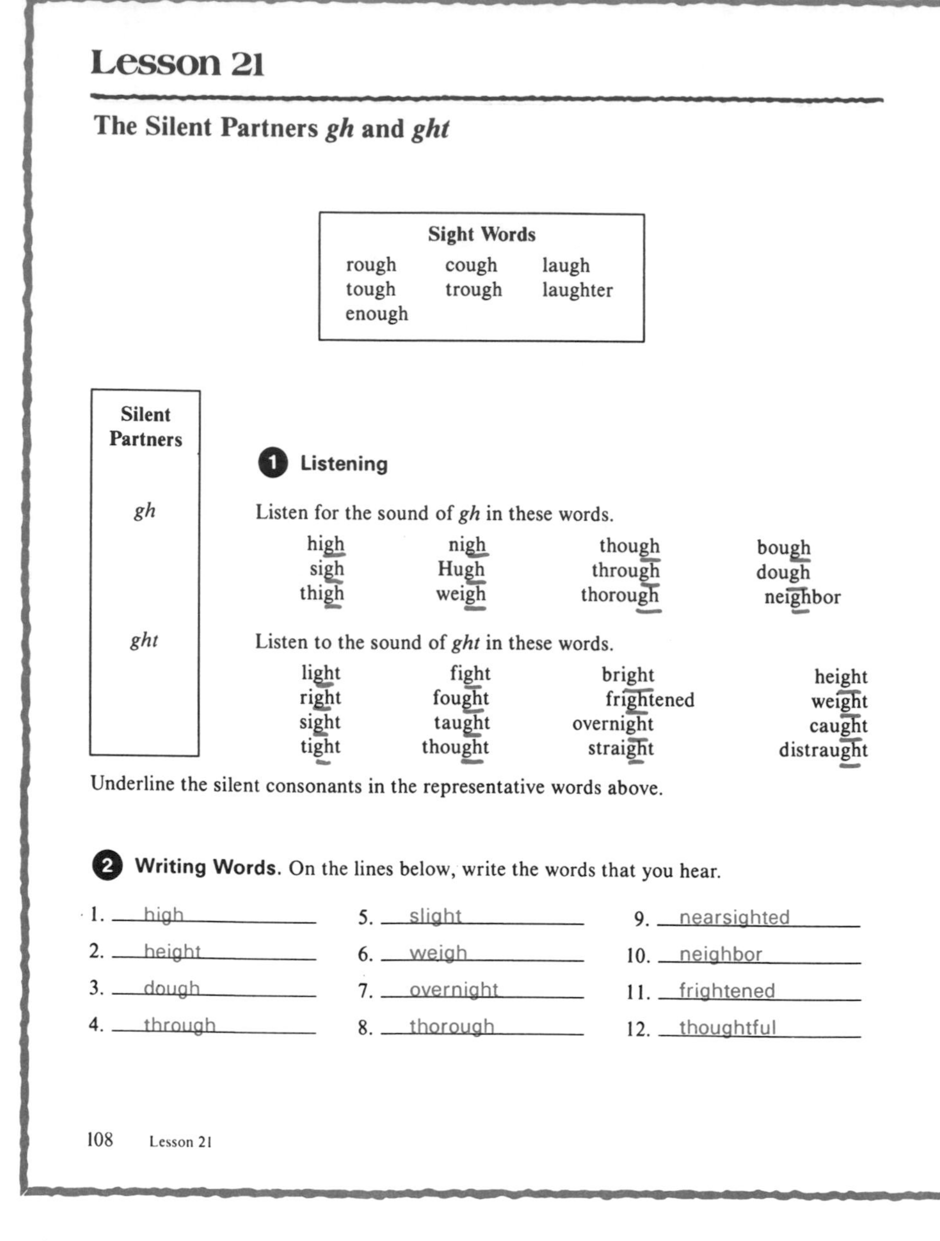

Lesson 21

The Silent Partners *gh* and *ght*

Sight Words		
rough	cough	laugh
tough	trough	laughter
enough		

Silent Partners
gh
ght

1 Listening

Listen for the sound of *gh* in these words.

high	nigh	though	bough
sigh	Hugh	through	dough
thigh	weigh	thorough	neighbor

Listen to the sound of *ght* in these words.

light	fight	bright	height
right	fought	frightened	weight
sight	taught	overnight	caught
tight	thought	straight	distraught

Underline the silent consonants in the representative words above.

2 Writing Words. On the lines below, write the words that you hear.

1. high	5. slight	9. nearsighted
2. height	6. weigh	10. neighbor
3. dough	7. overnight	11. frightened
4. through	8. thorough	12. thoughtful

Lesson 21

The Silent Partners *gh* and *ght*

Objectives

- **Silent Partners:** Learn to spell words with the silent partners *gh* and *ght*.
- **Sight Words:** Learn to spell *rough*, *tough*, *enough*, *cough*, *trough*, *laugh* and *laughter*. Use the sight words to complete sentences.
- **Silent Consonants:** Identify the silent consonants in the representative words.
- **Homonyms:** Select the correct spelling of homonyms based on context.
- **Compound Words:** Form compound words with one element given.
- **Using Words in Context:** Complete a paragraph by filling in designated words.
- **Writing Sentences:** Practice writing representative and sight words in context.
- **Composing a Story:** Write an original story using representative and sight words.

Sight Words

Teach the sight words using the methods described on pages 9-12 in the introduction to this book.

Note that in all of these words, the letters *gh* spell /f/. Most of these words were sight words in Books 1 and 2. They are being reviewed here to contrast the /f/ pronunciation of *gh* with the silent *gh* in the representative words in this lesson.

1 Listening

Talking about the sound made by silent letters can result in humorous questions or comments. If this happens, take advantage of it to increase students' enjoyment of language.

Introduce the words with the silent partners *gh* in the following way.

T: The first word is *high*. What letters make the sound /hī/?
S: *H-i-g-h*.

(If students respond *h-i*, remind them that *igh* was studied as a means of producing long *i* in Book 2. Then repeat the question.)

T: Good. What sound do the letters *gh* make?
S: None.
T: That's right. Both the *g* and the *h* are silent. Now, what letters produce the sound /ī/?
S: *I-g-h*.
T: Good. What letters make the *i* long?
S: *G-h*.
T: That's right. The *g-h* makes no sound of its own, but it does make the *i* long. Now, what letter spells the sound /h/?
S: *H*.
T: Good. What letters spell *high*?
S: *H-i-g-h*.
T: Right.

3 Using Sight Words. Fill in each blank with a sight word from this lesson. Use each word only once.

1. Herb's cold gave him a bad cough.
2. The horse took a long drink from the watering trough.
3. Norm sanded the rough wood until it was smooth enough to paint.
4. Ronald had a tough night, but he could laugh about it later.
5. The crowd's laughter was loud enough to wake the neighbors.

4 Dictionary Skills: Homonyms. Underline the correct word in each sentence below. Use a dictionary to check the meanings when necessary.

1. He chose the (right/write) word.
2. Who (ate/eight) the last piece of pie?
3. A mole is an animal that (boroughs/burrows) in the ground.
4. Chuck said he (might/mite) be able to do the job.
5. Is he really going to go (threw/through) with it?
6. Ralph kneaded the (doe/dough) and then let it rise.
7. Dwight went (straight/strait) to work on the problem.
8. The sailors were (taught/taut) to keep the rope (taught/taut).
9. Do you (know/no) who (rote/wrote) the Bill of (Rights/Writes)?
10. King Arthur established the (Knights/Nights) of the Round Table.
11. The committee has selected a (sight/site) for the (knew/new) building.
12. Nurses (way/weigh) babies when they are born to find their birth (wait/weight).

Lesson 21 109

Continue to introduce the other *igh* words following this pattern.

When introducing the rest of the *gh* words, point out that the *gh* is a signal that the vowels may not spell their most common sounds.

Follow the same steps to introduce the words with *ght*. Note the different pronunciation of *ei* in *height* and *weight*.

When all the representative words have been introduced, have students underline the silent consonants in each word.

Make sure that students know the meanings of all the representative words before going on with the lesson.

2 Writing Words

Instruct students to write the words that you dictate, which are found on the replica of the student page. Say each word, use it in a phrase or simple sentence, and say the word again.

3 Using Sight Words

This exercise gives students additional practice in writing the sight words from this lesson by using them to complete sentences.

4 Dictionary Skills: Homonyms

This exercise requires students to choose between homonyms. Some of the pairs, such as *taught* and *taut*, contain one word that is very common and one that is not. If students miss one of these, have them use both words of the pair in original sentences.

5 Word Building: Compound Words. Form compound words using each of the words below. Check the dictionary to see if the compounds you form are closed, hyphenated, or open.

1. sight ___foresight___
2. high ___highway___
3. dough ___doughnut___
4. through ___throughout___
5. weight ___heavyweight___
6. light ___lighthouse___
7. night ___nighttime___
8. rough ___roughhouse___
9. tight ___tightrope___
10. straight ___straightforward___

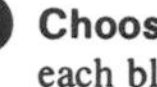

6 Choosing the Right Word. Write one of the words listed below in each blank. Use each word only once.

although though thought thorough throughout

Columbus was one of the early explorers who ___thought___ the world was round. Before he sailed on his voyage of discovery, he did a ___thorough___ job of preparation. Columbus discovered America ___although___ he had been looking for a passage to the Indies. News of his discovery soon spread ___throughout___ Europe. Even ___though___ he discovered the Western Hemisphere, the American continents were not named after Columbus.

7 Writing Sentences. On the lines below, write the sentences that you hear.

1. Bert is tough enough to get through the training.
2. Last night Hugh showed us a rough draft of his speech.
3. Dwight still has a cough from the cold he caught in March.
4. Bart thoroughly cleaned the trough before he brought the animals in from the pasture.
5. The girls fought to control their laughter, but they were laughing so hard they couldn't stop.

110 Lesson 21

5 Word Building: Compound Words

For most of the words given, there are several compound words available. Have the students check the dictionary if they are not sure whether a word is a valid compound word. Remind students that the given word can be either at the beginning or at the end of the compound word.

The words presented on the accompanying student page are examples. Accept all compounds listed in a dictionary.

6 Choosing the Right Word

The words *although*, *though*, *thought*, *thorough*, and *throughout* are often a source of trouble because they look so much alike. Before students begin this exercise, make sure they are pronouncing these words correctly.

Students should be able to produce the correct spelling of these words in context. If they have trouble with this exercise, it may be an indication of weaker-than-normal monitoring skills.

7 Writing Sentences

Instruct students to write the sentences that you dictate, which are on the replica of the student page. Give students a bit more time to write these sentences than you normally do for dictations. They contain several silent-partner words which may take students longer to recall.

These sentences give students an opportunity to write the sight words and some of the representative words in context. Note any specific errors that students make, and design additional words, sentences, or phrases for specific problems.

In addition to the silent partners covered in this lesson, the patterns found in these sentences include:
—homonyms (1)
—possessive pronouns (2 and 5)
—words ending in /chur/ (4)
—contractions (5)

8 Composing a Story. Write a story about the events pictured below. Use some of the representative words and sight words from this unit.

Lesson 21 111

8 Composing a Story

Discuss the illustrations with students before they begin to write their stories. They might enjoy developing their stories orally in small groups, but they should each write their own version of the story.

Suggest that they look through the word lists at the back of the book for words that they might use. Tell them to use extra paper if they need it.

Encourage students to look up words they aren't sure of after they finish writing. Remember that errors in words that haven't been studied yet shouldn't be treated negatively. Point out any parts of the word that are spelled correctly and praise the effort.

Review of Unit 6

The Silent Partners

1 Word Building. Write one of the silent partners below in each blank to make a word. Do not make the same word twice.

mb mn lm lk gn kn wr stle gh ght

1. ba lm	9. ru stle	17. gn ash
2. cha lk	10. tau ght	18. gn at
3. cli mb	11. thou gh	19. kn eel
4. desi gn	12. thou ght	20. wr en
5. hei ght	13. throu gh	21. wr estle
6. hi gh	14. to mb	22. kn ight
7. hy mn	15. wa lk	23. wr ite
8. pa lm	16. whi stle	24. kn ot

2 Review of the Related Words Strategy. Underline the silent consonant in each word below. Then write a related word in which the consonant is pronounced.

Word	Related Word	Word	Related Word
1. sign	signal	7. condemn	condemnation
2. column	columnist	8. resign	resignation
3. autumn	autumnal	9. hymn	hymnal
4. bomb	bombard	10. design	designation
5. solemn	solemnity	11. malign	malignant
6. crumb	crumble	12. soften	soft

112 Review of Unit 6

Review of Unit 6

The Silent Partners

Objectives

- **Word Building:** Add silent partners to word parts to form words.
- **Related Words:** Review the related words strategy for remembering silent consonants in words.
- **Silent Consonants:** Write words that contain designated silent consonants.
- **Homonyms:** Review designated homonyms by using them in original sentences.
- **Writing Sentences:** Practice writing representative and sight words in context.
- **Puzzle:** Review representative and sight words by completing a crossword puzzle.

1 Word Building

Have students add one of the silent-partner pairs or clusters to each word part to make a word. Encourage them to use all of the silent partners at least once. The answers given on the replica of the student page are examples. Accept all correctly spelled words.

2 Review of the Related Words Strategy

This exercise requires that students recall related words. If students have difficulty doing this, let them use their dictionaries.

Don't require the same related words that they found in Lessons 19 and 20. Any related word in which the silent consonant is pronounced will be acceptable.

Point out that most words in our language, especially the longer ones, have related forms. Making the connections between words is important for spelling success.

❸ Review of Silent Consonants

1. Write three words containing *mb* in which the *b* is silent.

______ ______ ______

2. Write three words containing *mn* in which the *n* is silent.

______ ______ ______

3. Write three words containing *lm* in which the *l* is silent.

______ ______ ______

4. Write three words containing *lk* in which the *l* is silent.

______ ______ ______

5. Write three words containing *gn* in which the *g* is silent.

______ ______ ______

6. Write three words containing *kn* in which the *k* is silent.

______ ______ ______

7. Write three words containing *wr* in which the *w* is silent.

______ ______ ______

8. Write three words containing *stle* in which the *t* is silent.

______ ______ ______

9. Write three words containing *gh* in which the *gh* is silent.

______ ______ ______

10. Write three words containing *ght* in which the *gh* is silent.

______ ______ ______

Review of Unit 6 113

❸ Review of Silent Consonants

This exercise reviews words that contain the silent consonant pairs and clusters covered in this unit. Answer words do not have to be from the representative words in these lessons. Accept all correctly spelled words that contain the required silent consonant.

4 Review of Homonyms. Use each of the homonyms below in a sentence.

1. knot ______
   not ______
2. ring ______
   wring ______
3. wait ______
   weight ______
4. threw ______
   through ______
5. sight ______
   site ______
6. knew ______
   new ______

5 Writing Sentences. On the lines below, write the sentences that you hear.

1. High up on the hill is an old wrecked castle.
2. Hugh knew the assignment had to be written by today.
3. The plumber found a comb wedged tightly in the pipe.
4. Don't condemn him for not knowing the right way to go.
5. Malcolm needs to know how much those chalkboards weigh.
6. When the kids stayed overnight with the neighbors, they were frightened by what they thought was a ghost.
7. In their fright, they ran straight into a patch of thistles and scratched their knees and knuckles.

114 Review of Unit 6

4 Review of Homonyms

This exercise reviews several of the more common homonym pairs covered in this unit. Students are to use each homonym correctly in an original sentence.

5 Writing Sentences

Instruct students to write the sentences that you dictate, which are on the replica of the student page. Give students a bit more time to write these sentences than you normally do for dictations. They contain several silent partner words which may take students longer to recall.

Note any specific errors. Design additional sentences, words, or phrases for specific problems.

In addition to the silent partners and sight words in this unit, patterns found in these sentences include:
—words ending in /səl/ (1 and 7)
—Silent *e* Pattern 1 (3)
—contractions (4)
—compound words (5 and 6)
—possessive pronouns (7)

6 Crossword Puzzle. Use the clues below to complete this crossword puzzle. Most of the answers are representative words or sight words from Unit 6 or words that contain silent letters.

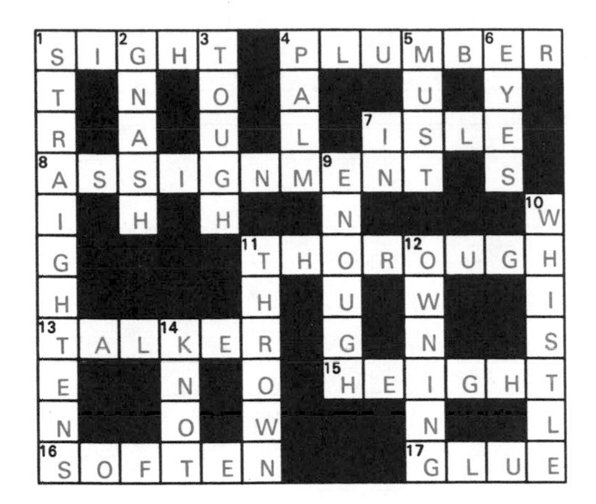

Across

1. Something that is seen: You are a ___ for sore eyes.
4. The person to call when your pipes leak
7. A small island
8. A task to be done; homework
11. Entirely complete: We gave the house a ___ cleaning.
13. A person who speaks a lot
15. The distance from the bottom to the top
16. To make soft
17. A sticky substance that holds things together

Down

1. Makes neat or straight
2. To grind the teeth
3. Not tender: This steak is ___.
4. A type of tropical tree
5. Has to: He ___ go home now.
6. What we see with
7. Opposite of out
9. Plenty; not too much
10. Blow through your lips: ___ while you work
11. A homonym of throne
12. Possessing
14. This ties two ropes together

6 Crossword Puzzle

Have students complete the crossword puzzle. Tell them that most of the answer words are representative or sight words from Unit 6. The clues are mostly definitions that rely on the students' general knowledge.

Allow them to use a dictionary if they want to. You might want them to work in pairs or small groups. If necessary, give them the following list of answer words and have them check off words as they use them.

assignment	palm
enough	plumber
eyes	sight
glue	soften
gnash	straightens
height	talker
in	thorough
isle	thrown
knot	tough
must	whistle
owning	

Unit 6 Tests

We recommend that you test your students on the representative words and sight words from Unit 6 before going on. The following are suggested lists of representative words and sight words from Unit 6. You may want to substitute other words to meet the needs of your students.

Dictate each word and use it in a simple sentence. Students should be able to spell 90 percent of the representative words and 16 of the 18 sight words correctly.

Representative Words	Sight Words
1. climb	1. threshold
2. condemn	2. reign
3. numb	3. aisle
4. calm	4. Lincoln
5. whistle	5. often
6. crosswalk	6. laugh
7. designing	7. trough
8. wrestle	8. cough
9. palm	9. psalm
10. talking	10. rough
11. kneeling	11. enough
12. wrapper	12. isle
13. knuckle	13. wherever
14. resign	14. laughter
15. wriggle	15. tough
16. dough	16. soften
17. thought	17. island
18. weigh	18. foreign
19. height	
20. thorough	

Review of Book 3

Objectives

- **Consonant Blends and Digraphs:** Review the blends and digraphs included in this text.
- **Word Building:** Add consonant blends and digraphs to word parts to form words.
  Form words by matching beginning and ending word parts.
- **Alternative Spellings:** Review various spellings of /shən/ by filling them in to complete words. Review various strategies for predicting the spelling of /shən/.
- **Root Words:** Identify root words of words that end in /shən/.
- **Patterns:** Review six patterns for adding endings.
- **Endings:** Add designated endings to words following six patterns.
- **Apostrophes:** Review various uses of the apostrophe.
- **Suffixes:** Review the suffixes *-er* and *-est* by adding them to words in context.
- **Homonyms:** Review designated homonyms by using them in original sentences.
- **Silent Consonants:** Review strategies for remembering silent consonants in words.
- **Puzzle:** Review representative and sight words by completing a crossword puzzle.

Consonant Blends and Digraphs

This chart presents the blends, digraphs, suffixes, and silent letter combinations presented in this text.

Review of Book 3

Consonant Blends and Digraphs

Beginning Blends Lessons 1-5 and 9-10	Digraphs and Suffixes Lessons 6-8	Ending Blends Lessons 11-18	Silent Partners Lessons 19-21
bl, cr			
cl, cr	ch, cian	ct	
dr			
fl, fr		ft	
gl, gr			gh, ght, gn
			kn
		ld, lf, lk, lm, lp, lt	lk, lm
		mp	mb, mn
		nd, ng, nk, nt, nce, nch, nge, nse	
pl, pr	ph	pt	
		rb, rd, rf, rk, rl, rm, rn, rp, rt, rce, rse	
sc, sk, sl, sm, sn, sp, st, sw, scr, shr, spl, spr, squ, str	sh, sion	sk, sp, st	stle
tr, tw, thr	th, tion, ture		
	wh		wr
		xt	

1 Word Building. Write one of the blends or digraphs above in each blank to form a word.

1. st air
2. sk ate
3. fr ee
4. th ere
5. br ight
6. bl ind
7. cl ock
8. sc ore
9. bo ld
10. ca stle
11. cha mp
12. fo rk
13. mi nd
14. se lf
15. wi lt
16. wo rse

For the most part, they are arranged alphabetically. The chart lets students see which blends begin syllables, which blends come at the end of syllables, and which consonants occur most often in blends.

Spend some time discussing the chart with students. Draw their attention to the many blends that begin with *s*. Point out that *l*, *r*, and *t* often occur as the second or third letter of a blend. Have students identify the blends and digraphs that can occur at both the beginning and the end of syllables.

1 Word Building

Have students form words by adding beginning blends or digraphs to the word families in numbers 1-8 and ending blends and suffixes to numbers 9-16. The answers given on the replica of the student page are examples. Many other combinations are possible. Accept all correctly spelled words.

Additional Exercise:

You might want to encourage students to write all the combinations they can think of using the blends and the word parts in this exercise. For instance, students might form *chair*, *flair*, and *stair* for number 1.

2 More Word Building. Add a word part from Column 2 to each blend or digraph in Column 1 to make a word. Write the words on the lines provided. Use each blend and digraph in Column 1 only once.

Column 1	Column 2
bl	ant
ch	ild
cr	ince
fr	ink
gr	ing
pr	irt
sk	ist
spr	ost
th	ough
tw	unch

Words

1. blink
2. child
3. crunch
4. frost
5. grant
6. prince
7. skirt
8. spring
9. though
10. twist

3 Words That End in /shən/. Fill in the correct spelling of /shən/ to complete each of the words below and answer the questions that follow.

1. direc tion
2. divi sion
3. atten tion
4. discus sion
5. addi tion
6. televi sion
7. pollu tion
8. objec tion
9. imagina tion
10. interrup tion
11. musi cian
12. magi cian

What is the most common way to spell /shən/ at the end of words? tion

What is the ending that indicates a person skilled in some work? cian

If you hear /k/ or /p/ before /shən/, how is the /shən/ spelled? tion

4 Root Words. On the lines below, write the root word of each of the words in Exercise 3.

1. direct
2. divide
3. attend
4. discuss
5. add
6. televise
7. pollute
8. object
9. imagine
10. interrupt
11. music
12. magic

Review of Book 3 117

2 More Word Building

In this exercise, students build words by matching and combining word parts. Instruct them to use each blend or digraph in Column 1 once. Accept all correctly spelled words.

3 Words That End in /shən/

The various spellings of /shən/ are reviewed in this exercise, as well as some of the strategies for predicting the spelling. Remind students that the only way to be sure of the spelling of /shən/ in any given word is to remember the spelling or look it up in the dictionary.

4 Root Words

This exercise reviews the relationship between the root words and the words formed by adding *-tion*, *-sion*, and *-cian*. Students can see the various ways the root words are changed when the suffixes are added.

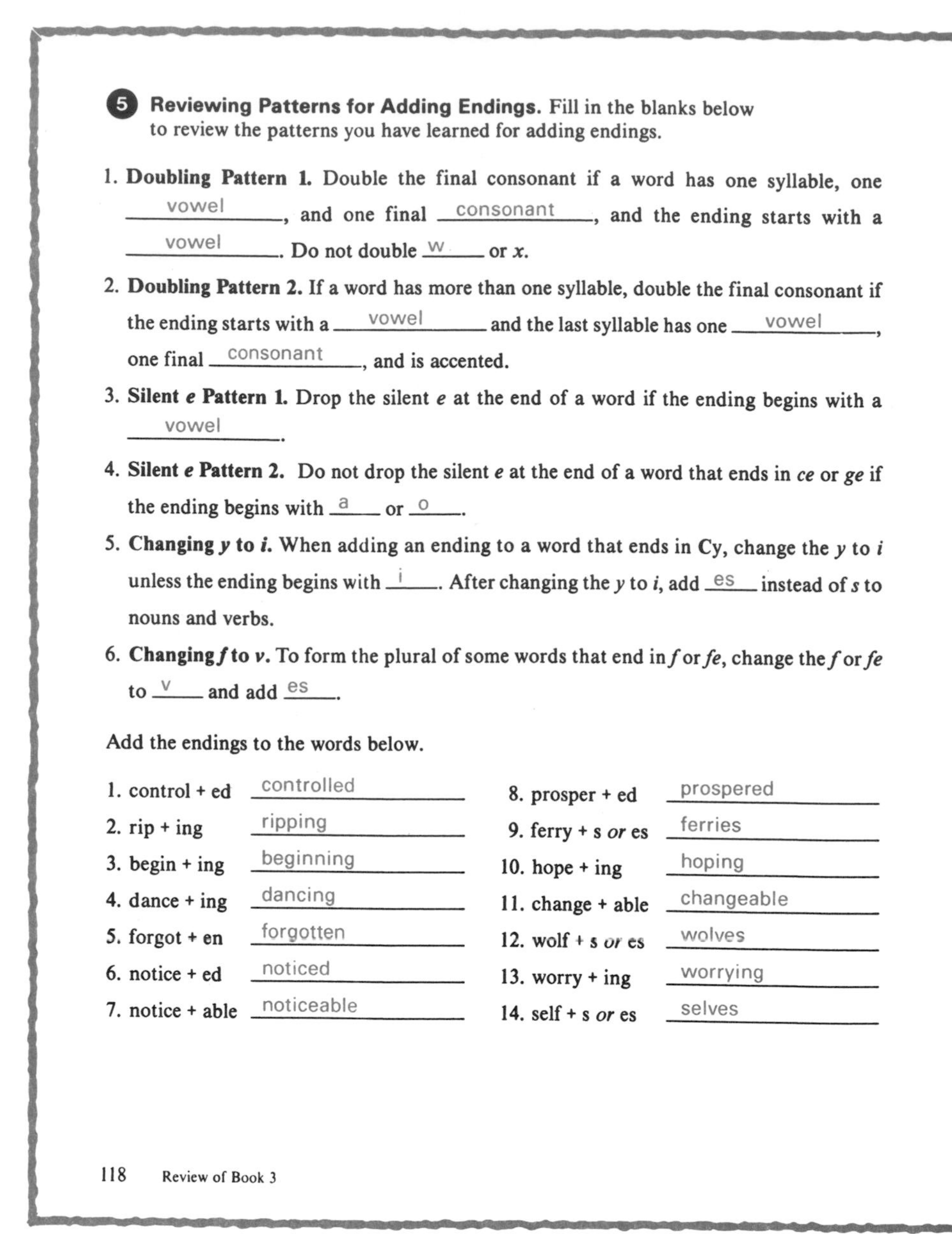

5 Reviewing Patterns for Adding Endings. Fill in the blanks below to review the patterns you have learned for adding endings.

1. **Doubling Pattern 1.** Double the final consonant if a word has one syllable, one vowel, and one final consonant, and the ending starts with a vowel. Do not double w or *x*.
2. **Doubling Pattern 2.** If a word has more than one syllable, double the final consonant if the ending starts with a vowel and the last syllable has one vowel, one final consonant, and is accented.
3. **Silent *e* Pattern 1.** Drop the silent *e* at the end of a word if the ending begins with a vowel.
4. **Silent *e* Pattern 2.** Do not drop the silent *e* at the end of a word that ends in *ce* or *ge* if the ending begins with a or o.
5. **Changing *y* to *i*.** When adding an ending to a word that ends in Cy, change the *y* to *i* unless the ending begins with i. After changing the *y* to *i*, add es instead of *s* to nouns and verbs.
6. **Changing *f* to *v*.** To form the plural of some words that end in *f* or *fe*, change the *f* or *fe* to v and add es.

Add the endings to the words below.

1. control + ed	controlled	8. prosper + ed	prospered
2. rip + ing	ripping	9. ferry + s *or* es	ferries
3. begin + ing	beginning	10. hope + ing	hoping
4. dance + ing	dancing	11. change + able	changeable
5. forgot + en	forgotten	12. wolf + s *or* es	wolves
6. notice + ed	noticed	13. worry + ing	worrying
7. notice + able	noticeable	14. self + s *or* es	selves

118 Review of Book 3

5 Reviewing Patterns for Adding Endings

The first section of this exercise reviews six patterns for adding endings that students have studied. The second section asks students to apply the patterns by adding endings to a variety of words.

Before students apply the patterns to the words in the second section, make sure the patterns are stated correctly in the first section.

6 The Apostrophe. Rewrite the phrases and sentences below adding the missing apostrophes.

1. Marys glasses — Mary's glasses
2. Two P.T.A.s were organized. — Two P.T.A.'s were organized.
3. She cant help it. — She can't help it.
4. the cities problems — the cities' problems
5. the childrens party — the children's party
6. I dont know. — I don't know.
7. several teachers classes — several teachers' classes
8. Arent you early? — Aren't you early?
9. his grandfathers beard — his grandfather's beard
10. Jack wouldnt like it. — Jack wouldn't like it.
11. todays project — today's project
12. cross your ts — cross your t's
13. the womens sewing group — the women's sewing group
14. those companies policies — those companies' policies
15. They havent been here. — They haven't been here.

7 Reviewing the *-er* and *-est* Suffixes. Fill in the blanks to complete the sentences below with the correct form of the word in parentheses. Remember to follow the spelling patterns you have studied.

1. (hungry) The baby was hungrier than I thought she would be.
2. (dry) The weather this year has been drier than last year.
3. (wet) Last April was the wettest month on record.
4. (juicy) Those oranges are juicier than the ones I bought.
5. (flat) That is the flattest tire I've ever seen.

Review of Book 3 119

6 The Apostrophe

This exercise reviews the various uses for the apostrophe that students have studied, including forming possessives, contractions, and plurals of letters and abbreviations. Students who are having difficulty with the possessive apostrophe should review the steps introduced in Lesson 1.

7 Reviewing the *-er* and *-est* Suffixes

This exercise reviews the *-er* and *-est* suffixes for showing comparison. Remind students to follow the patterns for adding endings that begin with vowels.

8 Reviewing Homonyms. Write a sentence using each of the following homonyms.

1. principal ______
2. principle ______
3. right ______
4. write ______
5. there ______
6. their ______
7. forth ______
8. fourth ______
9. threw ______
10. through ______
11. worn ______
12. warn ______

9 Review of Silent Consonant Strategies: Related Words and Mnemonics

Part A: For each of the words below, write a related word that contains a silent consonant.

1. hymnal	hymn	6. crumble	crumb
2. signal	sign	7. columnist	column
3. soft	soften	8. designate	design
4. solemnity	solemn	9. resignation	resign
5. bombard	bomb	10. condemnation	condemn

Part B: On the lines below, write a silent consonant word and a mnemonic that helps you remember how to spell it.

______ ______

120 Review of Book 3

8 Reviewing Homonyms

Encourage students to use their dictionaries if they need to verify the meanings of the homonyms. Evaluate students on their correct use of the homonyms in context and encourage them to spell other words as well as they are able.

9 Review of Silent Consonant Strategies: Related Words and Mnemonics

This exercise reviews two strategies for remembering silent consonants in words. If students have difficulty remembering related words, allow them to use their dictionaries.

10 **Crossword Puzzle.** Use the clues below to complete this crossword puzzle. Most of the answers are representative words or sight words from Book 3.

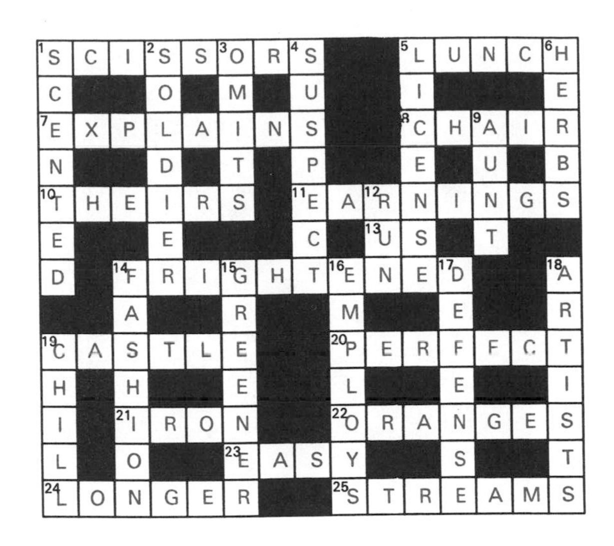

Across

1. Tools similar to shears
5. The meal between breakfast and dinner
7. Makes plain; gives reasons for
8. A piece of furniture to sit on
10. Belonging to them
11. Wages or profits
13. Abbreviation for the United States
14. Scared; afraid
19. A knight's home
20. Without any faults
21. The metal from which steel is made
22. Citrus fruits
23. The opposite of difficult
24. The opposite of shorter
25. Small rivers

Down

1. Perfumed: The soap is heavily ___.
2. A person who serves in the army
3. Leaves out; fails to include
4. Someone that police think committed a crime
5. A document showing legal permission: a driver's ___
6. Plants used to season cooking
9. Your parent's sister
12. The present tense of ran
14. Style: That suit is in the latest ___.
15. "The grass is always ___ on the other side of the fence."
16. Hires; gives work to
17. Protection: "The best offense is a good ___."
18. People who create fine art
19. Coldness: I felt a ___ in the air.

Review of Book 3 121

10 Crossword Puzzle

Have students complete the crossword puzzle. Tell them that most of the answer words are representative or sight words from Book 3. The clues are mostly definitions that rely on the students' general knowledge.

Allow them to use a dictionary if they wish. You might want them to work in pairs or small groups. If necessary, give them the following list of answer words and have them check off words as they use them.

artists
aunt
castle
chair
chill
defense
earnings
easy
employs
explains
fashion
frightened
greener
herbs
iron
license
longer
lunch
omits
oranges
perfect
run
scissors
scented
soldier
streams
suspect
theirs
U.S.

Book 3 Tests

We recommend that you test your students on the representative words and sight words from Book 3 before going on to Book 4. The following are suggested lists of representative words and sight words from Book 3. You may want to substitute other words to meet the needs of your students.

Dictate each word and use it in a simple sentence. Students should be able to spell 90 percent of the representative words and 22 of the 25 sight words correctly.

Sight Words

1. America
2. bird
3. bought
4. thread
5. science
6. restaurant
7. English
8. personal
9. guard
10. listen
11. century
12. work
13. Lincoln
14. worse
15. review
16. certain
17. scene
18. necessary
19. ocean
20. resource
21. whose
22. straight
23. cushion
24. billion
25. forth

Representative Words

1. blend
2. chance
3. built
4. trick
5. telephone
6. inch
7. thankful
8. assistant
9. disturb
10. skirt
11. perfect
12. scarce
13. license
14. film
15. context
16. heard
17. selfish
18. climb
19. condemn
20. calm
21. wrapper
22. thought
23. sign
24. through
25. complete
26. twitch
27. brain
28. agree
29. frog
30. crack
31. price
32. dropping
33. themselves
34. stable
35. response
36. smile
37. slap
38. flesh
39. donation
40. whistle
41. session
42. musician
43. ache
44. nature
45. squeal
46. strangest
47. describe
48. shrill
49. postmark
50. reverse

Word Families and Representative Words

Lesson 1

bl
black
blame
blank
blanket
blaze
blend
bless
blotch
blow
blown
blue
bluff

cl
claim
clap
class
clean
clear
cliff
clip
clock
clutch

fl
flag
flame
flare
flat
fled
flee
fleet
flight
fling
flock
fluid
fly

gl
glad
glare
glass
gleam
glide
glove
glow
glue
glum

pl
complain
complete
employ
explain
explore
place
plan
plane
please
pledge
plenty
reply

Lesson 2

br
braid
brain
brake
brave
breakfast
brick
bridge
broke
broken
brush
February
library

cr
crack
cradle
crankcase
crayon
crazy
cream
creek
creep
crop
cross
crossing
cry

fr
afraid
frame
France
free
freeze
Friday
friend
fright
frog
frost
froze
San Francisco

gr
agree
grab
grade
grain
grand
grapes
grave
grease
green
greet
griddle
grill

Lesson 3

pr
April
improve
practice
praise
pray
preach
preparing
present
president
pretty
price
pride
prize
problem
program
surprise

tr
country
entrance
pantry
track
trade
tragedy
train
trap
travel
treat
tree
trick
trim
trip
truck
truly

dr
address
children
drag
dream
dress
drive
drop
drove
drug
drum
dry
hundred

Lesson 4

st
stable
stack
stain
stake
state
stay
steam
steel
stick
stiff
still
stitch
stock
stuck
study
stuff

sp
inspect
respect
space
spade
Spain
Spanish
speak
special
spell
spend
spice
spill

sn
snack
snail
snake
snap
sneak
sneeze
sniff
snore
snow

sl
slap
sled
sleep
sleeve
slice
slick
slide
slipper

sm
small
smear
smell
smile
smoke
smudge

Lesson 5

sc
scab
scale
scar
scarce
scare
scarlet
scatter
scold
score
scout
scuff
scum

sk
skating
skiing
skillet
skin
skip
skirt
skull
sky

sw
swam
swear
sweat
sweep
sweet
sweetheart
swell
swim
swimming
swing
Swiss
switch

tw
between
tweed
twelve
twenty
twenty-five
twice
twilight
twin
twine
twinkle
twist
twitch

Lesson 6

sh
blush
flesh
shacks
shady
shall
she
shears
shining
shoe
should
shoulder
wish

tion
action
addition
attention
donation
fiction
imagination
inflation
occupation
pollution
station
transportation
vacation

sion
admission
discussion
division
expression
permission
profession
session
television

cian
beautician
optician
magician
musician

Lesson 7

ph
alphabet
microphone
phobia
phone
phony
photograph
physical
physician
telephone

ch as /ch/
bleach
chain
chance
cheap
check
cheese
child
merchant
reach
rich
speech
teacher

ch as /k/
ache
anchor
chorus
character
chemical
Christmas
stomach
technical
technician

ture
adventure
agriculture
feature
fracture
lecture
mixture
nature
picture

Lesson 8

th as /th/
anything
athletic
bath
both
thank
thick
think
thirsty
thirteen
thunder
tooth
truth

th as /*th*/
brother
smooth
than
that
their
themselves
there
these
this
though
thus
together

wh
awhile
what
wheel
when
where
whether
which
whichever
whip
whistle
white
why

Lesson 9

str
strap
strange
stream
street
stretch
strike
string
strong
struck

scr
describe
description
inscription
scrap
scrape
scratch
scream
screen
scrub

spl
splash
splatter
splendid
splice
splinter
split

spr
sprain
spray
spree
spring
sprinkle
spry

Lesson 10

squ
squad
squall
squander
square
squat
squeak
squeal
squeamish
squeeze

shr
shrank
shred
shrill
shrimp
shrine
shrink
shrivel
shrub
shrunk

thr
three
threw
thrill
thrive
throat
throng
through
throw
thrust

Lesson 11

nd
bandage
bind
defend
find
fond
found
grandfather
handful
offend
pretend
remind
respond

nt
argument
aunt
cent
complaint
faint
important
infant
payment
pint
rent
sent
spent

nce
absence
announce
chance
convince
dance
difference
entrance
experience
fence
insurance
once
ounce
pronounce
residence
sentence
since

nse
defense
expense
license
offense
response
rinse
sense
tense

Lesson 12

ng
hanger
longing
nothing
rang
ring
rung
singer
standing
strongly
tongue
wrong
young

nk
bank
crankcase
ink
sank
shrank
sink
sunken
thankful
trunk

nch
branch
brunch
bunch
clinch
French
inch
lunch
munch
pinch
ranch
workbench
wrench

nge
angelfish
arrangement
challenge
changeable
cringe
exchange
fringe
hinge
lounge
lunge
orange
strangely

Lesson 13

mp
bump
camping
company
damp
empty
impish
pumpkin
slumping

sp
clasp
crisp
gasp
grasp
lisp
wasp

st
assist
cost
crust
dentist
fast
first
mostly
past

sk
ask
basketball
brisk
desk
disk
dusk
mask
risking

Lesson 14

lt
adult
belt
built
colt
consult
difficult
felt
melting
quilt
result
saltiest
wilt

ld
behold
bold
building
child
field
foretold
golden
rebuild
shoulder

lm
elm
film
helm
helmet
overwhelm
realm

Lesson 15

lk
bulk
buttermilk
elk
hulk
silk
sulking

lp
gulps
help
helper
pulp
pulpiness
scalp

lf
engulf
golfing
gulf
selfish
shelf
wolf

Lesson 16

ct
act
affect
attract
connect
contract
direct
district
elected
exact
intellect
object
perfect
react
strict
suspect
verdict

ft
draft
drift
gift
handicraft
left
lift
raft
sift
soft
swift
theft
thrifty

pt
abrupt
accept
adapt
adopt
apt
attempt
concept
Egypt
interrupt
kept
prompt
slept

xt
context
next
text

Lesson 17

rd
aboard
afford

chord
cord
forward
hardly
heard
herd
hurdle
regard
third
toward

rm
alarm
disarm
firmly
germ
harm
midterm
storm
swarming
transform
uniform
warm
warmth

rn
adornment
barn
burned
concern
cornfield
fern
lantern
torn
tornado
turn
warn
worn

rb
adverb
curb
disturb
garb
garbage
proverb
suburb
superb
verb

rf
dwarf
scarf
surf
surface
surfboard
turf

Lesson 18

rt
alert
comfort
dirty
expert
forty
inverted
part
port
quart
shirt
skirt
sport

rl
curl
girl
hurl
purl
snarl
swirl
twirling
unfurled
whirl

rk
dark
fork
housework
network
park
pork
postmark
remark

rse
coarse
converse
course
curse
discourse
disperse
endorse
hoarse
horse
nurses
purse
rehearse
reimburse
reverse
sparse
verse

rce
divorced
enforce
fierce
force
pierce
reinforce
scarce
scarcely

rp
burp
chirping
harp
sharp

Lesson 19

mb
bombshell
climb
comb
crumb
dumb
dumbwaiter
lamb
limb
numb
plumber
thumbnail
womb

mn
autumn
column
condemn
condemned
hymn
solemn

lm
balm
calm
embalm
Malcolm
palm
qualm

lk
chalk
crosswalk
folk
folklore
stalk
talk
walk
yolk

Lesson 20

gn
align
assign
assignment
benign
campaign
designing
gnash
gnat
gnaw
resign
sign

kn
knee
kneeling
knew
knit
knob
knock
knot
know
knowledge
known
knuckle
reknown

wr
awry
playwright
wrapper
wreck
wriggle
wring
wrinkle
wrist
write
written
wrong
wrote

stle
bristle
bustle
castle
hustle
jostle
rustle
thistle
whistle
wrestle

Lesson 21

gh
bough
dough
high
Hugh
neighbor
nigh
sigh
thigh
thorough
though
through
weigh

ght
bright
caught
distraught
fight
fought
frightened
height
light
overnight
right
sight
straight
taught
thought
tight
weight

Sight Words

Sight Word	Lesson Number
aisle	20
America	1
billion	1
bird	17
bought	15
bruise	2
build	2
captain	14
century	1
cereal	4
certain	4
chef	7
chocolate	3
clerk	13
corps	18
cough	21
cruise	2
cushion	6
down	15
earn	17
England	12
English	12
enough	21
example	16
fashion	6
finger	12
folk	15
food	3
foreign	20
forth	14
fruit	2
ghetto	16
ghost	16
guard	11
guardian	11
herb	17
hoist	13
house	1
indict	16
interview	11
iron	1
island	20
isle	20
juice	2
laugh	21
laughter	21
learn	17
Lincoln	20
linger	12
listen	15
longer	12
look	15
machine	7
million	1
moist	13
natural	7
necessary	4
ocean	6
often	19
onion	3
pearl	18
personal	13
personnel	13
psalm	19
psychologist	7
psychology	7
refrigerator	3
reign	20
resource	18
restaurant	11
review	11
rough	21
salad	3
sample	16
scene	5
scent	5
schedule	5
school	5
science	5
scissors	5
sergeant	14
shrewd	10
shriek	10
simple	16
soften	19
softener	19
soldier	14
source	18
spaghetti	3
spatula	7
spread	9
squirrel	10
straight	9
strength	9
sugar	6
suit	2
sure	6
suspicion	6
sword	17
Thomas	8
thought	8
thread	10
threshold	19
tough	21
trough	21
view	11
warp	18
wear	8
weather	8
wharf	17
wherever	19
whoever	8
whose	8
word	17
work	13
world	14
worm	17
worse	18
worth	14
yolk	15
younger	12